OECD Urban Studies

Housing Affordability in Cities in the Czech Republic

This work was co-funded by the European Union via the Structural Reform Support Programme (PA grant agreement SRSS/2019/036). The views expressed herein can in no way be taken to reflect the official opinion of the European Union.

Please cite this publication as:
OECD (2021), *Housing Affordability in Cities in the Czech Republic*, OECD Urban Studies, OECD Publishing, Paris, *https://doi.org/10.1787/bcddcf4a-en*.

ISBN 978-92-64-42970-3 (print)
ISBN 978-92-64-41789-2 (pdf)

OECD Urban Studies
ISSN 2707-3432 (print)
ISSN 2707-3440 (online)

Photo credits: Cover © Ministry of Regional Development of the Czech Republic.

Corrigenda to publications may be found on line at: *www.oecd.org/about/publishing/corrigenda.htm*.

Preface

At the onset of the COVID-19 crisis and episodes of lockdown, governments have focused on keeping people safe at home. The pandemic has brought longstanding housing challenges and inequalities to the fore. Never has it been more striking that affordable housing constitutes both a basic human need and a key driver of people's well-being. Housing does not only provide a shelter with fundamental services such as water and electricity, but it also determines people's access to jobs, infrastructure, and public goods. Housing is a critical component of household wealth and contributes to people's health, work-life balance and social connections. Ensuring quality and affordable housing for all helps reduce inequalities and ensure communities are socially integrated. Housing is therefore critical to build more resilient and inclusive cities.

Over the past couple of decades, housing affordability has become one of the most pressing challenges in cities, where house prices have often outpaced national averages. The Czech Republic is no exception. Despite constant efforts from the government to meet the increasing need for housing, many low- and middle-income households are getting priced out of cities.

In 2019, the Czech Republic requested support from the European Union's Structural Reform Support Programme to help reform its National Housing Strategy. The European Commission teamed up with the OECD to provide expertise and guidance. A few months after the project started, the global COVID-19 crisis broke out, revealing – and often aggravating – many of the housing challenges that the Czech Republic was already struggling with before the pandemic, such as housing insecurity, insufficient housing supply and homelessness. Urgent and decisive action was needed to protect the most vulnerable urban households, better match housing supply and demand, and upgrade the quality of existing housing.

While the full extent of the COVID-19 fallout still remains uncertain at the time of writing this report, efforts to put the world back on the path to sustainable growth are offering an unprecedented momentum to drive forward long-term policies that expand affordable and adequate housing for all. There is a window of opportunity right now for the EU Member States to make good use of the European Union's Renovation Wave and in particular of the Affordable Housing Initiative.

We encourage the national and local governments in the Czech Republic and beyond to leverage housing policy to shape a healthier, safer and brighter future for all in cities.

Daniela Grabmüllerová

Deputy Minister, Section of Coordination of EU Funds and International Relations

Ministry of Regional Development Czech Republic

Lamia Kamal-Chaoui

Director, Centre for Entrepreneurship, SMEs, Regions and Cities

OECD

Nathalie Berger

Director for Support to Member States' Reforms

Directorate-General for Structural Reform Support

European Commission

Foreword

The report *Housing Affordability in Cities in the Czech Republic* comes at a critical time. Across OECD economies, housing costs have been absorbing an increasing share of household income, reaching 31% for the average middle-income household. The Czech Republic is no different in this respect, with house prices rising by 43% since 2013, almost twice as fast as in the OECD on average. Many people are therefore increasingly struggling to afford decent housing, particularly in cities where demand is outpacing supply.

The COVID-19 crisis has shone a harsh light on chronic underlying challenges that were already clogging housing markets before the pandemic, such as growing housing insecurity and obstacles to housing construction. While national and local authorities across the OECD have taken emergency measures to protect their most vulnerable residents from the immediate impact of the crisis, including through shelter for the homeless, freezing rents for social housing, and suspending evictions, longer-term action is needed.

As part of the OECD Horizontal Housing Initiative, this report investigates housing challenges in, and solutions for, cities in the Czech Republic. Building on an innovative survey of more than 1 800 Czech municipalities, the report aims to guide the 2021 reform of the Czech Housing Strategy. Concerted action from national and local governments will be critical to expand access to quality housing for all to shape more sustainable and resilient cities.

Acknowledgements

The report *Housing Affordability in Cities in the Czech Republic* was produced by the OECD Centre for Entrepreneurship, SMEs, Regions and Cities (CFE), led by Lamia Kamal-Chaoui, Director, as part of the Programme of Work of the Regional Development Policy Committee (RDPC) and its Working Party on Urban Policy (WPURB).

The project was funded by the European Union via the Structural Reform Support Programme and was implemented in co-operation with the Directorate-General for Structural Reform Support of the European Commission.

The OECD is grateful to Daniela Grabmüllerová, Marie Mohylová and Katarina Husarova from the Ministry of Regional Development of the Czech Republic for the excellent collaboration. Warm thanks also are due to the cities of Pilsen (Plzeň) and Olomouc for their input during the onsite mission in January 2020, as well as to the stakeholders from the government, the Czech National Bank, the Czech Statistical Office, civil society, academia and business representatives that contributed data and information throughout the project.

The report was drafted by Camille Viros and Klara Fritz, Economists/Policy Analysts, under the supervision of Soo-Jin Kim, Head of the Urban Policies and Reviews Unit, and Aziza Akhmouch, Head of the Cities, Urban Policies and Sustainable Development (CITY) Division of the CFE. The report also benefitted from valuable contributions and comments from Abel Schumann, Matteo Schleicher and Jaebeum Cho, Economists, under the supervision of Rudiger Ahrend, Head of the Economic Analysis, Data and Statistics Division.

The report was approved for declassification at the 29th session of the OECD Working Party on Urban Policy (3-4 May 2021) under cote [CFE/RDPC/URB(2021)12].

The report was prepared for publication by Pilar Philip and François Iglesias and edited by Eleonore Morena.

Table of contents

Tables

Figures

Boxes

Follow OECD Publications on:
http://twitter.com/OECD_Pubs
http://www.facebook.com/OECDPublications
http://www.linkedin.com/groups/OECD-Publications-4645871
http://www.youtube.com/oecdilibrary
OECD Alerts
http://www.oecd.org/oecddirect/

Abbreviations and acronyms

AHI	Affordable Housing Initiative (European Union)
CNB	Czech National Bank
CZK	Czech Koruna
DSTI	Debt Service-To-Income
DTI	Debt-To-Income
EC	European Commission
ELENA	European Local ENergy Assistance
ESF	European Social Fund
EU	European Union
EUR	Euro
EU-SILC	European Union Statistics on Income and Living Conditions
FUA	Functional Urban Area
GDP	Gross Domestic Product
H+T	Housing and Transportation Affordability Index
MMR	Ministry of Regional Development (*Ministerstvo pro místní rozvoj*) of the Czech Republic
PIT	Personal Income Tax
REIT	Real Estate Investment Trust
RMO	Olomouc City Council (*Rada města Olomouce*)
SISF	State Investment Support Fund
VAT	Value-Added Tax

Executive summary

Against the backdrop of the COVID-19 pandemic, the Czech national government has taken a number of emergency measures to help maintain people in their homes, for example by introducing a mortgage forbearance, one of the most common support measures across OECD countries, which has helped alleviate immediate challenges in housing affordability. Whilst the full extent of the effects of the COVID-19 crisis on housing affordability remains to be seen, the pandemic has reinforced the urgency of tackling pre-existing housing challenges, such as insufficient housing supply and increased housing insecurity for many households. To alleviate the housing affordability challenge in cities and use housing as a tool to shape a more sustainable and inclusive urban paradigm beyond the COVID-19 crisis, national and local governments in the Czech Republic could implement both direct and indirect policy instruments. Direct policy instruments target housing affordability specifically, for example by providing social housing and allocating housing benefits. Indirect policies can also affect housing supply and housing affordability, for example through building regulations, land use, spatial planning and fiscal instruments. In co-operation with the Ministry of Regional Development of the Czech Republic, the OECD carried out a survey of 1 877 Czech municipalities in August/September 2020 to collect data on the housing market and housing policies at the municipal level – the first of its kind in terms of scale and reach.

Key findings

- **Following the post-1989 massive privatisation of the housing stock, including at the municipal level, homeownership has been the main type of housing tenure in the Czech Republic**. The transition of the Czech Republic to a market economy since 1989 entailed massive privatisation of the housing stock. Faced with strict rent regulations and a lack of financial and human resources to ensure housing maintenance, municipalities privatised a major part of their housing stock. Homeownership is currently the dominant type of tenure in the Czech Republic (75% of households vs. 43% for the OECD average). The private rental market is relatively limited (18% of households vs. 25% for the OECD average).
- **Many Czech households are struggling to access affordable housing, especially in cities**. House prices in the Czech Republic have soared faster than household disposable income, especially in Czech cities where house prices have often risen at a faster pace than the national average. While the rise in house prices may benefit the large share of Czech homeowners, it has made it even harder for newcomers, especially the young, to get a foot on the housing ladder. With rents also rising and with relatively limited supply, the private rental market offers few alternatives for people struggling to find affordable housing.
- **Despite the COVID-19 crisis, structural drivers pushing housing demand up in Czech cities are likely to remain**. As has been the case in many countries, strong demand for housing in Czech cities has been driven by many factors, including strong economic growth and rising real wages until 2020, favourable lending conditions, changes in household composition, and population ageing. In cities, these factors have been further boosted by faster population growth reflecting migration from rural areas and from abroad. The increase in tourism, driving an intensified use of

short-term rental platforms, has also led to a surge in rental prices and a shrinking rental stock for domestic residents.

- **Czech cities are facing a consistent shortage of housing supply**. The high and growing demand for housing in Czech cities has not been met by a sufficient increase in housing supply. Construction activity has not kept up with its pre-2009 levels, and zoning and land use planning do not steer housing development where it is most needed. The shortage of qualified construction workers and the complexity of the building permit process pose further constraints on private sector housing supply.
- **The housing stock in Czech cities is often old and needs energy efficiency improvements**. While building insulation and heating equipment have improved in recent years, building energy efficiency in the Czech Republic remains relatively poor compared with other OECD countries. Increasing dwellings' energy efficiency would not only improve housing quality but also have a substantial impact on overall housing affordability through reduced energy bills.
- **Social housing provision does not meet the needs of all low-income and vulnerable households**. The social housing stock in the Czech Republic is too small to meet the demand of all low-income and vulnerable households, with municipalities facing obstacles to increasing supply. Additionally, municipalities have complete autonomy in deciding how they use the housing stock they own, define the conditions in which they rent it out, choose the eligibility criteria for social housing or allocate social housing within the eligible population. This can generate inequalities across municipalities and a lack of clarity in the allocation of social housing, which in turn may prevent some households that need it the most from accessing social housing.
- **Barriers to the housing market leave some vulnerable groups in substandard housing**. As private rental accommodations at market prices have become financially inaccessible for many Czech households and availability of municipal social housing is limited, many households have no choice but to turn to housing with substandard conditions, such as the so-called "dormitories".
- **The Czech Housing Strategy provides a dedicated national framework for housing affordability policy in the Czech Republic**. It focuses on three priorities: i) affordability of adequate housing; ii) stability of the housing market; and iii) quality of housing. However, its implementation is hampered by several factors, including a lack of a clear definition of "social housing", the multiplicity of actors involved in the housing policy framework and limited financial resources.
- **Direct policy instruments to support housing affordability exist but have limitations**. Several programmes are in place to help specific groups access homeownership. However, supporting homeownership may not be enough to solve the affordability issue for low-income families and can even be counterproductive in some cases by hampering labour mobility. Housing benefits exist but eligible households may not necessarily claim them because they might not be aware of their availability, the administrative process used to allocate the housing allowance is too complicated and recent adjustments to the formula determining the income taken into account to assess eligibility have resulted in more complexity.
- **Municipalities tend to lack a local housing policy framework and intermunicipal co-ordination on housing policy remains limited**. Czech municipalities generally do not have a dedicated housing policy, do not monitor local housing prices or set explicit targets for housing development. In addition, most municipalities do not co-ordinate with each other on housing policies, partly due to the fiscal framework, which leads to competition between municipalities.

Key policy recommendations

- **Steer housing development toward urban areas where demand for housing is high**. In order to increase affordable housing supply where it is most needed and reduce vacant housing in areas where demand is low, housing development needs to target urban areas where housing demand is high.
    - Provide clear national regulations to guide local planning policies on where housing development should occur or not.
    - Use local land use planning instruments to encourage private sector construction of affordable housing. Where housing demand is high, the use of developer obligations within local land use planning policies, such as inclusionary zoning, could be broadened.
    - Ensure compact, transport-oriented development to reduce auxiliary costs of housing in cities. The costs associated with long car commutes can outweigh cheaper housing costs associated with more peripheral locations. Transit-oriented development also contributes to avoiding segregation and facilitates access to public services and economic opportunities.
    - Manage publicly owned land strategically and use it for the provision of affordable housing where possible. This can be done, for example, through joint development agreements with private developers or not-for-profit housing providers.
    - Monitor the effectiveness of the national reform of the building permit process. While the current reform of the Building Act is expected to accelerate and streamline permit-granting procedures for the average citizen and the larger investor, the impact of this reform should be monitored to make sure this is the case.
- **Provide more alternatives to homeownership, including rental housing**
    - Encourage municipalities to scale up rental housing in their planning policies. Considering the social housing shortage and given that rental housing is the only solution for most low-income households and the "squeezed" middle class that do not have access to social housing and are unable to afford homeownership, public policies at all levels of government should encourage the construction and provision of rental housing.
    - Introduce a national deposit scheme and rent guarantees to support vulnerable households in accessing the private rental market and reduce risks of rent loss for landlords in order to increase housing supply.
    - Reform housing co-operatives and engage non-governmental actors, by supporting non-profit institutions as housing providers to further promote the co-operative housing sector.
- **Reinforce the supply of social housing**
    - Increase public investment in social housing. Reducing the shortage of social housing will require greater public investment by national and local governments.
    - Introduce a national social housing policy framework that guides municipal housing. National guidelines need to steer an equitable distribution of the available social housing stock and give priority to those who need it the most while incentivising municipalities to increase their housing stock.
    - Remove barriers to access social housing, such as deposit requirements and debt restrictions that prevent the most vulnerable households from accessing social housing, by exploring other options such as a national legal basis allowing municipalities to withhold rent payments from the housing allowance in the event of repeated failure to pay rents.

- **Ensure that the most vulnerable households have access to adequate housing**
  - Simplify the application process for housing allowances and subsidies.
  - Strengthen the regulation of dormitories to better protect residents. While national and local governments should ultimately aim at eliminating the need for dormitories, short-term regulations have to strike a balance between increasing the protection of residents and avoiding the closure of dormitories.
- **Adopt a metropolitan-area approach to housing (including social housing), transport and spatial planning**. Developing joint housing, transport and spatial plans at the metropolitan level (i.e. at the functional urban area level) can help overcome the consequences of administrative fragmentation and steer housing development to locations that are well connected to public transport and close to employment centres. The national government should continue to support intermunicipal co-operation and joint service provision, including through financial incentives.
- **Leverage fiscal and financial instruments more effectively to support housing affordability**
  - Make more use of the power of municipalities to increase property tax rates in order to increase revenues and invest more in housing, while introducing means-tested exemptions to avoid adding to low-income households' tax burden.
  - Introduce differentiated property tax and tax breaks to incentivise more efficient land use through higher-density housing development, discourage low-density housing and promote brownfield developments.
  - Shift to a value-based property tax, and/or introduce other various "value-capture" mechanisms linked to specific public infrastructure projects to allow for a more equitable sharing of the increase in property value between private individuals, businesses and municipalities.
  - Tap into current and upcoming external sources of financing such as those from the European Union (EU), in particular to encourage a more sustainable and socially responsible housing stock (e.g. EU Renovation Wave and the Affordable Housing Initiative).

Assessment and recommendations

Introduction

While the long-term impacts of the COVID-19 pandemic still remain uncertain at the time of writing this report, the crisis has brought to the fore many of the longstanding issues that the Czech Republic was facing in the field of housing, such as housing insecurity, homelessness and inequalities, as observed in many other OECD countries (OECD, forthcoming[1]). Such challenges are even more acute in cities and urban areas, where property and rental prices have often increased faster than in the Czech Republic in general and the share of households overburdened by housing costs or the share of those who live in overcrowded dwellings are higher. To enrich the analysis, the OECD, in co-operation with the Ministry of Regional Development of the Czech Republic or *Ministerstvo pro místní rozvoj* (MMR), carried out a survey of 1 877 Czech municipalities in August/September 2020 to collect data on the housing market and housing policies at the municipal level. The survey will hereinafter be referred to as the OECD-MMR housing survey. The survey covered all municipalities within functional urban areas (FUAs) of more than 50 000 inhabitants in the Czech Republic, as well as the municipalities within the FUAs of Jablonec and Mladá Boleslav (see Annex A for further details on the administration of the survey).

Key findings

Following the post-1989 massive privatisation of the housing stock, including at the municipal level, homeownership is the main type of housing tenure in the Czech Republic

Following the transition from the communist regime to a market economy starting from 1989, the housing stock in the Czech Republic went through a massive movement of privatisation. Faced with strict rent regulation and a lack of financial and human resources for housing maintenance, municipalities privatised a major part of the housing stock that had been transferred to them. As a result, as in many other former communist countries in Central and Eastern Europe, homeownership has been the dominant type of tenure in the Czech Republic, with 75% of Czech households owning their accommodation (well above the OECD average of around 43%). The private rental market is relatively limited, with only 18% of Czech households renting their dwelling from the private rental sector (compared with 25% in OECD countries on average (OECD, 2020[2])). The share of households that rent their dwelling from the subsidised market (state-owned or other) is also very low, at only 1.4% of all households. Social rental dwellings only account for 0.4% of the total number of dwellings in the Czech Republic – a very low share compared with other OECD countries (e.g. 20% in Austria, 7.6% in Poland and 4.0% in Hungary (OECD, 2020[2])).

Many Czech households are struggling to access affordable housing, especially in cities

House prices have increased faster than household disposable income

Since reaching their lowest post-financial crisis levels in 2013, house prices in the Czech Republic have increased sharply and now largely exceed their pre-crisis level. Between the first quarter of 2013 and the second quarter of 2020, real house prices rose by 43.1%, a much higher growth rate than in OECD countries, where, on average, real house prices increased by 24.9% over the same period. In 2018 alone, house prices increased by 7.1% in the Czech Republic – one of the highest growth rates among EU countries (just below the growth rates observed in Hungary, Latvia and Portugal). Estimates from the Czech National Bank indicate that the Czech housing market was overvalued by around 25% at the end of 2019 (CNB, 2020[3]).

House prices in the Czech Republic have soared faster than household disposable income, making housing increasingly unaffordable for first-time buyers, renters and those who have to move from cheap areas into more expensive ones for work reasons for example. Czech households need to save more than 11 years of gross annual salaries to buy a standardised new dwelling of 70 square metres, compared to approximately 9 years in Latvia and 7 years in Hungary and Poland (Deloitte, 2020[4]).

House prices have risen faster in cities than in the rest of the Czech Republic

While house price growth has varied considerably across regions, it has generally been higher in cities than in the rest of the Czech Republic. Across the Czech Republic, the larger the municipalities in terms of population size, the more expensive the housing, suggesting that there is a price premium for living in cities. In all 13 regions of the Czech Republic, house prices are consistently higher in municipalities that have more than 50 000 inhabitants than in smaller municipalities. Prague is the most expensive city in the Czech Republic and according to the Czech Statistical Office, Prague also recorded the strongest price growth (41.7%) since 2010 for all types of real estate among all regions in the Czech Republic. Following Prague, Brno is the second most expensive regional capital, followed by Ceske Budejovice, Hradec Kralove and Pilsen.

The private rental market offers few housing alternatives due to increases in rental prices

While the rise in house prices may benefit the large share of Czech households that own their dwelling (due to the rise in the value of their assets), it means that purchasing a home remains out of reach for most newcomers to the housing market. As rents have also been increasing, the private rental market offers few alternative options to homeownership. Between the second quarter of 2019 and the second quarter of 2020, rent prices in the Czech Republic increased by 3.7%, which is lower than the 4.3% increase in house purchase prices over the same period but remains one of the highest growth rates among European and OECD countries.

Living in cities imposes a heavy financial burden on Czech households

Housing-related expenditure is the single-largest expenditure of Czech households for all income groups. In 2018, Czech households spent on average 26.5% of their total expenditure on housing – which is higher than the OECD average of 22.3% and one of the highest shares among all OECD countries. According to the European Union Statistics on Income and Living Conditions (EU-SILC), the financial burden of housing costs for Czech households is particularly high for vulnerable groups: households at risk of poverty (i.e. those with an income below 60% of the median national income), single people, people aged 65 and above, and single parents. Two in 3 low-income renters in the Czech Republic spend more than 40% of their disposable income on housing-related costs (the so-called "housing cost overburden rate"), often due to high costs of utilities (electricity, gas, water, etc.) (OECD, 2020[2]). The share of households overburdened by housing is also higher in cities than in the rest of the country, with the overburden rate increasing with the degree of urbanisation.

Drivers pushing housing demand up in Czech cities are likely to withstand the COVID-19 crisis

Many factors have been driving the demand for housing in cities

Strong demand for housing in Czech cities has been driven by many factors, including: strong economic growth and rising real wages until 2020; favourable lending conditions; changes in household composition; and population ageing. While such factors influencing house prices are national, housing markets are by definition influenced by their location and involve a range of specific local factors. Cities are popular locations and attract people who want to benefit from the availability of jobs, education, lifestyle and cultural opportunities, as well as urban infrastructure, public goods and services.

Even though the Czech Republic is less urbanised than high-income countries on average (22% of the population lives in cities, 37% in towns and semi-dense areas and 41% in rural areas, compared with 49%, 27% and 24% respectively in high-income countries on average) (OECD/EC, 2020[5]), the Czech Republic has continued to urbanise over the past decade. Its population living in FUAs, i.e. a city and its commuting zone, has increased faster than in the country overall (+4.5% between 2009 and 2019 compared to 1.8% in the Czech Republic over the same period). Faster population growth in Czech cities is due to inflows from rural areas to the main cities, as well as inflows of migrants from abroad who tend to settle in urban areas and students – both Czech and from abroad – who come to study in renowned universities. Some Czech cities are also very attractive to investors and the increase in tourism and intensified use of short-term rental platforms have put more pressure on house prices in the past few years. While the COVID-19 crisis put a sudden halt to touristic activities in the Czech Republic, most drivers pushing housing demand up in Czech cities are likely to withstand the crisis, since structural drivers such as demographic trends and attractiveness of urban areas continue to be prevalent and economic growth is expected to resume in 2021.

Housing demand has been increasing faster in urban peripheries than in urban centres

While the population has been increasing faster in FUAs than in the rest of the Czech Republic, this has been driven by an increasing share of the urban population living outside urban centres. Between 2009 and 2019, in all Czech FUAs except for the city of Most, the population increased faster in the commuting zones of the FUAs than in their core cities, indicating a phenomenon of urban sprawl. This has significant environmental, economic and social consequences, including higher emissions from road transport (as sprawling cities are characterised by larger distances between homes and jobs, more likely to be covered by car) and higher costs of providing key public services (such as water supply, electricity and public transport, which are more expensive to provide in sprawling rather than compact areas).

Czech cities face a shortage of housing supply

Construction activity has not caught up with previously high levels from before the 2009 financial crisis

Such high and growing demand for housing in Czech cities has not been met by a sufficient increase in housing supply. Construction activity (measured by the number of started and completed dwellings) declined after the financial crisis and has yet to recover. Furthermore, according to calculations from the MMR, the housing stock decreased between 2011 and 2017, as the number of new dwellings did not compensate for the wear and tear of old buildings or the change from residential to commercial use. According to the 2020 OECD-MMR housing survey, about a third of municipalities that responded built no new housing over the past five years. Furthermore, the COVID-19 pandemic put a halt to all construction projects in the spring of 2020, which will lead to a sharp decrease in completed dwellings for the year of 2020 compared to previous years.

Construction activity does not happen where it is most needed, while zoning and land use planning do not steer development towards urban areas where housing demand is high

The OECD-MMR housing survey shows that housing construction does not focus on high-priced areas, where it would be most needed. There is no indication that municipalities with higher price levels have increased construction activity, which suggests that the growth in demand (reflected in higher prices) has not been buffered by an increase in supply. In contrast, many municipalities with low price levels experienced considerable housing development. In these municipalities, there is therefore a risk that this excess in housing development creates undesired side-effects in terms of vacancy rates and urban sprawl.

In several OECD countries, local zoning and land use planning policies often hamper housing construction and limit housing supply, contributing significantly to high housing costs (OECD, forthcoming[1]). In the Czech Republic, however, there is little indication of that happening, since municipalities have zoned large areas of undeveloped land for residential development. In municipalities covered by the OECD-MMR housing survey, an average of 79 m²/inhabitant of greenfield land is zoned for development in local master plans. This corresponds to approximately 15% of the current built-up area of the municipalities covered by the survey. Yet, the Czech planning system does not seem to contribute to steering housing development in areas with high prices. There is no relationship between the amount of greenfield land per inhabitant within a municipality that is zoned for development and the level of house prices. On average, municipalities with very low price levels have zoned the same amount of land for development as municipalities with very high housing price levels, which suggests that the planning system does not contribute to reversing the pattern of untargeted housing development. This lack of planning direction is also apparent when considering that the average amount of undeveloped land suitable for development owned by municipalities is significant. According to the OECD-MMR housing survey, municipalities own about 51 m²/inhabitant of undeveloped land that is suitable for housing construction, which is equivalent to approximately 9% of their built-up area.

Private sector housing supply faces several constraints

Other factors may explain the shortage of housing supply, including a shortage of qualified construction workers and managers, making it difficult for developers and local governments to find contractors and led to lengthy construction times and higher construction costs. Furthermore, the complex building permit process generates delays in obtaining building permits and licences, creating bottlenecks in housing construction. The Czech Republic ranks 157th out of 190 countries surveyed in the World Bank's Doing Business 2020 survey in terms of "dealing with construction permits". It takes 21 procedures and 246 days to build a warehouse in the Czech Republic, whereas in OECD countries on average, it takes 12.7 procedures and 152.3 days (World Bank, 2019[6]). According to the OECD-MMR housing survey, municipalities responded that the main constraints for private developers were the cost of infrastructure provision, the lack of available land and the lack of infrastructure capacity. In line with the aforementioned World Bank data, the complicated and lengthy building permit process also ranked high on the list of constraints.

The housing stock in Czech cities is often old and needs energy efficiency improvements

Almost all Czech households have access to basic facilities since 99.3% of dwellings in the Czech Republic offer private access to an indoor flushing toilet, which is more than the OECD average of 95.6%.

The Czech Republic also fares relatively well compared with other European countries when it comes to the basic quality of dwellings.

However, people living in cities tend to have less space than people who live in rural areas or towns and suburbs. In 2018, the average number of rooms per person was 1.4 in cities, compared with 1.5 in towns and suburbs and 1.6 in rural areas. This was slightly lower than the European average of 1.6 rooms per person who lives in a city. A relatively high share of Czech households also lives in overcrowded dwellings: 12.2% of the Czech households, slightly above the OECD average rate of 10.9%. Tenants are also much more likely to live in overcrowded housing than homeowners (OECD, 2020[2]).

An additional issue related to housing quality in cities in the Czech Republic lies in the physical deterioration of real estates, including buildings and neglected public spaces. According to the 2011 Population and Housing Census, the average age of occupied residential buildings in the Czech Republic was 52.4 years for multi-unit buildings and 49.3 years for family houses, which is older than the average age of buildings in the EU (Office of the Government, 2019[7]). Although the State Investment Support Fund has implemented several programmes to encourage repairs and modernisation of housing, the number of dwellings for which renovation (requiring building permits) has started or been completed has been decreasing over the past decade.

Renovation to improve dwellings' energy efficiency is another key dimension of housing quality, which can have a substantial impact on housing affordability. While energy efficiency improvements have occurred in the past years (mostly due to improvements in insulation of buildings, refurbishment of old buildings and improvements in heating equipment), energy intensity per floor area of residential space heating (i.e. the energy used to heat one square metre) is still high and remains one of the highest among OECD countries (after correcting for temperatures).

Barriers to the housing market leave some social groups in substandard housing

As private rental accommodations rented at market prices have become financially inaccessible for many Czech households and availability of municipal social housing is limited, many households have no choice but to turn to substandard housing, such as dormitories. Dormitories are flats or rooms, most often in private buildings, where residents do not have standard rental contracts, do not receive a local residence permit and frequently pay overpriced rents for small and low-quality spaces (e.g. shared kitchen, shared sanitation facilities, overcrowding, badly insulated with energy leaks), poorly maintained by their private owners. People who have been living in this type of alternative housing often face stigma and discrimination when they later attempt to access the private rental market, which locks them in precarious housing in the long term. These facilities frequently provide housing to migrant workers and marginalised population groups, such as the Roma, who are often excluded from regular housing markets.

Within the 758 municipalities that provided information on dormitories as part of the OECD-MMR housing survey, there are 555 privately-run dormitories, which are home to approximately 0.7% of the population in these municipalities. However, these numbers could be underestimated given the difficulties in collecting reliable data on dormitories, in particular due to their complicated ownership structures

In addition to people living in substandard conditions or inadequate housing, there are also a number of people who are either homeless or at risk of becoming homeless. According to the Ministry of Labour and Social Affairs, in 2016, there were around 68 500 homeless people (of which 21 230 adults and 2 600 minors are "roofless", according to the 2019 census) and 119 000 are at the risk of becoming homeless across the Czech Republic.

Social housing provision does not meet the needs of all low-income and vulnerable households

The social housing stock in the Czech Republic is too small to meet the demand of all low-income and vulnerable households

In the Czech Republic, social housing is understood as municipally owned housing that is allocated based on criteria decided by the municipality. As discussed previously, the social housing stock in the Czech Republic is very small, accounting for only 0.4% of the total number of dwellings in the country – a very low share compared with other OECD countries. However, this very low number could well be the consequence of an unclear definition of what constitutes social housing in the Czech Republic. Even after excluding outliers, municipalities participating in the OECD-MMR housing survey indicated that they own 8.7% of their total housing stock and provide it to residents at below-market rates. Social housing provision by non-governmental organisations also remains very rare. It exists only in 5% of all surveyed municipalities and the number of housing units provided tends to be low (3.6 housing units per 10 000 inhabitants). Approximately half of these units were built in the past five years, indicating that this is a relatively novel approach that could have the potential to grow in the future.

According to the OECD-MMR housing survey, more than half of the municipalities covered by the survey own housing (57%). However, this percentage varies significantly according to the size of the municipality, ranging from less than 40% among very small municipalities to close to 90% of large municipalities. Furthermore, more than 90% of municipalities that own housing make at least part of their housing stock available as social housing and 73% provide their entire housing stock at below-market rents.

The shortage of social housing is visible in the long waiting lists of aspiring tenants who apply for social housing. Among municipalities that allocate access to social housing through waiting lists, the median wait time is 24 months but, in 18% of municipalities, it can even reach 60 months or longer. In light of such a shortage of social housing, it comes as no surprise that 35% of municipalities that responded to the OECD-MMR housing survey indicate that increasing the stock of social housing is a policy priority. However, only 15% of all municipalities built any housing between 2015 and 2019.

Allocation of social housing varies across municipalities

Social housing in the Czech Republic is mostly provided by municipalities, which have complete autonomy in deciding how to use the housing stock that they own. They can choose to rent it out at market rates, just as any private rental housing provider, or to provide social housing at reduced rents to specific population groups. If municipalities choose the latter option, they set eligibility criteria autonomously and determine the conditions at which they rent it out (such as rent levels, deposit requirements, etc.). Municipalities are not only free to choose how much social housing they provide and at what price, they can also determine who is eligible and how to allocate housing within the eligible population. In the absence of national binding guidelines, the allocation of social housing to households in need by individual municipalities is sometimes opaque and can prevent some households that need it the most from accessing social housing. Selection criteria may include: time spent on a waiting list; social criteria such as age, family size, single-parent households and people belonging to specific marginalised communities such as the Roma community; special arrangements for the disabled and elderly; and the amount of a contribution tenants make to the municipality, without a clear and systematic record system of these contributions.

Beyond designating eligible groups for social housing, municipalities can introduce further requirements that can limit access to social housing for some population groups. Especially relevant in this context are deposit requirements and a ban on individuals who have a debt with the municipalities. Both requirements can prevent very low-income households from accessing social housing even though they are most urgently in need.

Municipalities face obstacles in the development of social housing

According to the OECD-MMR housing survey, local governments own considerable amounts of undeveloped land that is suitable for housing development (approximately 9% of their built-up area). Although Czech municipalities own significant amounts of developable land, there is a lack of investment in new social housing in general in the Czech Republic. In 2018, central government spending on social rental housing (encompassing both direct provision of social rental housing and subsidies to non-governmental social rental housing providers) in the Czech Republic was only 0.01% of gross domestic product (GDP) – this is about 10 times less than the average of public spending by national governments of OECD countries for which data is available (OECD, 2020[2]).

Several reasons could explain the low level of investment in new social housing. First, much of the municipally owned land suitable for development is located in small municipalities. According to the OECD-MMR housing survey, 71% of all municipally owned land belongs to municipalities that have less than 1 000 inhabitants. Such small municipalities might not have the capacity needed to provide affordable housing on the land. Moreover, house prices in municipalities that own larger amounts of land per capita tend to be lower than house prices in municipalities that own less land, reducing the incentives to build more affordable housing. Furthermore, the current legislative framework in the Czech Republic puts the responsibility of providing affordable housing and allocating social housing on municipalities, which may deter municipalities from making politically risky and unpopular decisions. When municipalities do intend to develop social housing, they are faced with a number of obstacles, the most important bottleneck being the shortage of funds (both from their own financial resources and from the national state).

The Housing Policy Strategy provides a dedicated national framework for housing affordability policy in the Czech Republic

The Czech Republic has a specific national housing policy in place, called the *Housing Policy Strategy in the Czech Republic Till 2020* (hereinafter the Housing Strategy). The Housing Strategy focuses on three priorities: i) affordability of adequate housing; ii) stability of the housing market; and iii) quality of housing (Ministry of Regional Development, 2011[8]). This framework offers a comprehensive outline of the policy instruments available in the Czech Republic, including support for homebuyers and homeowners (subsidies to households to facilitate homeownership, tax relief for access to homeownership, support to finance housing regeneration), the housing allowance for tenants and homeowners, the housing supplement for social assistance recipients and subsidies for the development of affordable rental housing. Initially established in 2011 and set to be renewed in 2021, it follows a clear time horizon and is updated on a regular basis to keep abreast of new trends and developments on the housing market. Furthermore, its focus on housing quality as well as quantity constitutes an important effort to adopt a holistic approach to housing affordability, especially as the housing stock in Czech cities is often old and in need of energy efficiency improvements.

However, its implementation faces legal, institutional and financial challenges

Despite the existence of this concrete national housing policy framework, some limitations are hampering its effective implementation. One major limitation to the Housing Strategy is the lack of legal definition for terms as important as "social housing", which has led to an "underregulated" and inefficient social housing sector (de Boer and Bitetti, 2014[9]). A national framework for social housing does exist, in the form of the Social Housing Policy Strategy of the Czech Republic 2015-2025, which was approved in 2015 and is under the responsibility of the Ministry of Labour and Social Affairs. While it outlines the objectives of the Czech government in terms of social housing, it does not constitute legislation on social housing, it is distinct from the Housing Strategy with no clear and systematic connection with it and the term "social housing" remains used in different ways throughout official documents.

Furthermore, the high number of actors within the system complicates the national housing policy framework. At the national level, housing policy is primarily led by the Ministry of Regional Development. However, other ministries administer certain housing benefits and related programmes without clear co-ordination mechanisms. For example, prominent actors include the Ministry of Labour and Social Affairs (social security allowance for housing, contribution for renovations for disabled people), the Ministry of Finance (building savings scheme, tax relief measures), the Ministry of the Environment (energy efficiency renovations scheme) and the Ministry of the Interior (integration of asylum seekers). At the local level, municipalities are responsible for housing provision, including affordable and social housing. They also have competency over grant allocation and distribution, urban planning and zoning.

Another obstacle is a lack of financial resources, both at the national and local levels. The government's spending to support housing affordability in the Czech Republic is generally low compared to other OECD countries. In 2017, state expenditure on housing was only 0.39% of GDP, including about 0.18% spent on housing allowances (below the OECD average of 0.25%).

Direct policy instruments to support housing affordability exist but have limitations

Two main housing policy instruments in the Czech Republic are: i) the housing allowance, paid to low-income families and individuals who cannot afford housing at market prices (i.e. housing costs exceed 30% of the household's sum of incomes after deduction of contributions to health and social insurance and income tax); and ii) the housing supplement, paid to the lowest-income households. These are both distributed by the Ministry of Labour and Social Affairs. However, unawareness of the benefit, the complicated administrative process to receive it and recent adjustments to the formula determining the income taken into account to assess eligibility resulting in more complexity can lead to some "non-uptake" of the housing allowance among eligible households.

Multiple policy instruments encourage homeownership, mostly via demand-side subsidies, including grants and tax reliefs, buy-to-rent schemes and relief for distressed mortgages, with several programmes targeting specific groups run by the State Investment Support Fund (former State Housing Development Fund). However, supporting homeownership may not solve the affordability issue for low-income families, and some policies to encourage homeownership may in fact be counterproductive. For example, mortgage interest tax deductions for homeownership may disproportionately benefit high-income households. Furthermore, homeownership can hinder labour mobility and be a driver of structural rigidities, partly because high transaction costs associated with the purchase or sale of property result in homeowners being less mobile than renters. This can be an issue especially in the current context of the economic fallout from the COVID-19 crisis and the rise in unemployment.

Municipalities tend to lack a housing policy framework and intermunicipal co-ordination on housing policy remains limited

At the local level, Czech municipalities generally lack a housing policy framework. A comprehensive and solid housing policy framework is important to set strategies that address housing shortages, monitor local housing construction trends and prices, as well as to set explicit targets for housing development. According to the OECD-MMR housing survey however, 63% of municipalities that answered the survey indicated they had no housing strategy. Another 70% of municipalities had no explicit quantitative and/or qualitative targets for housing development in place and 75% failed to monitor housing prices on a regular basis. Finally, over one-third (36%) of municipalities did not monitor local housing construction trends. Even when there is a housing strategy, it is not embedded within a broader spatial planning framework. In addition, 89% of municipalities indicated that there was no intermunicipal co-ordination on housing policies.

This lack of intermunicipal co-ordination on housing policies may be related to the lack of incentives for co-operation in the subnational financial framework in the Czech Republic. Subnational governments in the country are mostly financed through a mix of shared taxes (personal and corporate income tax, and value added tax), as well as grants and transfers from the central government. Although progressive decentralisation from 1989 onwards has given Czech municipalities more competencies, municipalities have little fiscal autonomy compared to other OECD countries. Since population size is the main determinant of the revenues that municipalities receive from the national government through the tax-sharing formula, municipalities in the Czech Republic tend to compete with one another for the population in order to increase their revenue base and the size of government transfers. This may lead to suboptimal land uses such as the promotion of sprawling housing developments for which it is costly to provide services and deliver and maintain infrastructure (OECD, 2017[10]).

Key policy recommendations

Steer housing development toward urban areas where demand for housing is high

Provide clear national and regional guidance to local planning policies

In order to increase affordable housing in urban areas where it is most needed and reduce vacant housing in areas where demand for housing is low, housing development needs to target urban areas where housing demand is high. This requires national, regional and local action. National planning frameworks need to provide clear regulation to guide local planning policies on where housing development should occur or not. Where necessary, these guidelines should also have binding power on local governments. In turn, municipalities should strive to adapt their planning policies more effectively to local housing markets. Where demand for housing is high, planning policies should encourage high-density housing development. Where housing demand is low, local zoning should be more restrictive to prevent overdevelopment and its associated negative fiscal and environmental consequences.

Use local land use planning instruments to encourage private sector construction of affordable housing

The use of developer obligations within local land use planning policies could be broadened. In particular, many OECD countries have successfully used inclusionary zoning (i.e. the requirement on developers to provide a share of housing units in new developments as affordable rental units) to improve housing affordability in the most expensive cities. For example, most major cities in Germany use inclusionary zoning and related instruments extensively. In 2020, the city of Frankfurt passed a new regulation that not only requires the provision of 30% affordable rental units in greenfield developments but also the provision of 10% affordable owner-occupied units, 15% co-operative units and 15% free-market rental units.

While such regulation is especially suitable for urban areas where housing demand is high, it needs to be used more carefully in contexts where housing demand is less high, as it may stifle housing supply and increase prices if it reduces incentives for developers to build housing. In cities with lower housing demand levels, requirements such as those introduced by Frankfurt could obstruct new housing development. To avoid such unintended consequences, it is important that inclusionary zoning and similar requirements are adapted to the local context.

To enable local governments to use inclusionary zoning, the national government needs to provide the corresponding legal framework. Local governments, in turn, need to develop the expertise and build up the administrative capacity within their planning departments to use the instruments at their disposal effectively. In particular, local governments will need to strengthen their capacity to develop effective regulatory plans and use their planning powers to engage proactively with developers to steer housing development in the desired direction.

Minimum parking requirements should also be abolished to reduce construction costs and encourage housing construction within urban centres. Such requirements tend to drive construction costs up, especially in densely populated city centres where the cost of providing the parking space often exceeds the price of the car that uses it (Litman, 2016[11]). They also generate high social costs as they take up valuable public space and encourage car use over public transport (Shoup, 2005[12]).

Ensure compact, transport-oriented development to reduce auxiliary costs of housing in cities

Transport-oriented development offers an important tool to reduce the auxiliary costs of housing. Housing that is located far away from city centres and disconnected from public transport networks requires long car commutes. The costs associated with these commutes can outweigh cheaper housing costs associated with more peripheral locations.

One option to steer housing location towards transport-oriented development is the use of integrated indices that take both housing and transport costs into account, such as the Housing and Transportation (H+T) Affordability Index used in the United States. Planners can use such an index to encourage the construction of affordable housing in neighbourhoods with higher land costs but lower transport costs, and to target public transport investments (Guerra and Kirschen, 2016[13]). The index can also help individuals make informed decisions about where to find the most affordable housing, taking into account transport costs.

Beyond improving housing affordability, transport-oriented development yields a range of other benefits for low-income households. For example, it can contribute to avoiding segregation and facilitating access to public services and economic opportunities that might otherwise remain out of reach for these households due to a lack of suitable transport options.

Manage publicly owned land strategically to provide affordable housing where possible

In places where housing demand is already high, municipalities should aim at using this land for the provision of affordable housing, for example by entering into joint development agreements with private developers or not-for-profit housing providers. Where housing demand is currently low or where publicly owned land cannot be developed for other reasons, municipalities should treat publicly owned land as a strategic resource that can help them provide affordable housing in the future. Where possible, infrastructure investments and other urban planning decisions should help enable the future use of municipal land for affordable housing development. Likewise, decisions to sell public land should be made only after taking a long-term perspective on the potential value of the land for the municipality.

Monitor the effectiveness of the national reform of the building permit process

The complexity and time-consuming process for obtaining a building permit in the Czech Republic is an obstacle to more housing development. The current ongoing reform of the Building Act and related laws (which are expected to take effect in 2023) is an attempt to alleviate such challenges and accelerate the building process, especially by integrating separate processes (including the issuance of binding opinions, zoning decisions and building permits) into a single procedure managed by a one-stop-shop regional building and construction authority. The renewed building permit process aims to give citizens the opportunity to obtain a building permit within one year of submitting an application, including a possible appeal against a decision and judicial review. While this reform is expected to accelerate and streamline the permit-granting procedures for the average citizen and the larger investor, the planned change will be demanding on the management and internal organisation of work within the regional building and construction authorities. A key condition for the successful setup and operation of the new system is the overall digitisation of administrative proceedings and documents for issuing decisions. The impact of this reform should be monitored to make sure the procedures are accelerated and streamlined, both for individual citizens and for large developers.

Provide more alternatives to homeownership

Encourage municipalities to scale up rental housing in their planning policies

Sufficient stock of affordable rental housing is a key component of an affordable housing market. Rental housing is the only solution for low-income households and for the "squeezed" middle class that do not have access to social housing but are unable to afford mortgages to purchase housing. Moreover, rental housing is usually available at much shorter notice than owner-occupied housing and social housing.

Although the stock of rental housing in the Czech Republic is low by international standards, municipalities give the provision of rental housing a very low priority. Only 11% of all surveyed municipalities indicated that increasing the stock of rental housing is a policy priority, even though 46% of all municipalities were in favour of increasing the supply of privately built housing.

Given the importance of rental housing for low-income and middle-income households and the low stock of rental housing in the Czech Republic, public policies at all levels of government should encourage the construction and provision of rental housing. National incentives to increase the stock of rental housing must be better structured to allow municipalities to leverage them. Municipalities often lack the resources to take advantage of existing programmes (such as the Guarantees programme for rental apartment development) as they cannot fund construction upfront.

The Czech Republic could take further inspiration from many OECD countries where national governments have implemented specific measures to support the rental market. Such measures include rent guarantee and deposit schemes, and minimum quality regulations for rental dwellings. For example, rent guarantees and deposits can be structured to reduce risks of rent loss for landlords in order to increase the supply of private rental housing or to support tenants who cannot afford to pay the initial deposits for rentals. Given the inability of some low-income households to pay such deposits, national deposit schemes could play an important role, in particular by supporting households currently living in dormitories to move into regular housing.

Reform housing co-operatives and engage non-governmental actors to reach housing affordability objectives

Housing co-operatives became popular in the post-war Czech Republic because most construction costs could be financed by state loans and more efficient housing structures (i.e. multi-unit buildings, prefabricated buildings) could be constructed by several households pooling resources rather than by any one household alone. Today, residents are legally allowed to sell the right to live in housing co-operatives. This is due to provisions enacted to curb the grey market trading of housing shares.

EU state aid rules in relation to the support of housing outside of social housing are rather strict, complicating the ways the national government can support non-governmental actors in the provision of affordable housing. The EU Urban Agenda Housing Partnership's guidance paper on EU regulation and public support for housing stipulates that "non-financial measures are also available to authorities to support investments in affordable, adequate and social housing without being labelled as state aid under EU rules. E.g.: Support the creation and capacity of institutions and organisations that will contribute to social and affordable housing such as not-for-profit investors, Community Land Trusts, housing cooperatives and public companies" (2017[14]). Such non-financial measures like supporting non-profit organisations as housing providers could be leveraged to promote further the co-operative housing sector.

Reinforce the supply of social housing

Increase public investment in social housing

Reducing the shortage of social housing will require greater public investment by the national and local governments. Currently, municipal housing construction is low, even though it is a political objective for many municipalities to increase social housing provision. As a consequence, long waiting lists for social housing persist and a significant number of people have little choice but to live in dormitories and other forms of substandard accommodation. Additional financial support from the national government for social housing development is critical to provide more affordable housing. National support to municipalities should also be made available ahead of construction to avoid that short-term financing constraints deter municipalities from undertaking social housing development.

Introduce a national social housing legislative framework that guides municipal housing

In addition to the objectives already set out in the Social Housing Policy Strategy of the Czech Republic 2015-2025, clear national legislative guidelines on social housing could help better co-ordinate social housing policies conducted by municipalities. The current lack of national guidelines has created an uneven landscape across the Czech Republic, in which social housing stocks, prices and eligibility requirements vary widely among municipalities. National guidelines can help steer a more equitable distribution of the available social housing stock and give priority to those who need it the most. Such guidelines should include a legal definition of social housing that enables all levels of government to regulate social housing effectively. Moreover, they should ensure co-ordination across municipalities within FUAs (see OECD definition of FUAs (Dijkstra, Poelman and Veneri, 2019[15])) to take into account the fact that the need for and availability of social housing are uneven across municipalities. Lastly, national guidelines should provide municipalities with financial incentives to continuously enlarge their social housing stock.

Remove barriers to access to social housing

Deposit requirements and restrictions on debt prevent some eligible households from accessing social housing, thereby excluding many of the poorest households that would need access to social housing most urgently. In order to prevent households living in social housing from persistently failing to pay their rent, other options should be explored. For example, the national government could create a legal basis that allows municipalities to withhold rent payments from the housing allowance if social housing tenants repeatedly fail to pay their rents.

Ensure the most vulnerable households have access to adequate housing

Simplify the application process for housing allowances and subsidies, and ensure it remains accessible to those who need them the most

The complex administrative procedures to access housing allowances and subsidies can be prohibitive for some households. Simplifying the housing allowance system to reach more people is, therefore, a positive step. However, to be eligible for such benefits, households must have already established a residence for a number of months, which means that those who are unable to access such housing in the first place often remain out of the system even though they are the most vulnerable (e.g. those living in temporary accommodation, including dormitories). The simplification of the housing allowance system must therefore be part of a broader package of measures to protect the most vulnerable households.

Strengthen the regulation of dormitories to better protect residents

National regulations of dormitories should be strengthened to better protect residents and improve their living conditions. Although tenants in rental housing are typically granted some statutory protections, people living in dormitories usually do not benefit from them. Not only do tenants of dormitories lack security of tenure but there is a higher risk of eviction for groups such as the Roma community in particular.

While national and local governments should ultimately aim at eliminating the need for dormitories altogether, short-term regulations have to strike a balance between increasing the protection of residents and avoiding the closure of dormitories. As dormitories often constitute a last-resort option for residents, regulations that would lead to their closure would leave residents worse off unless viable alternative forms of accommodation exist. National regulations of dormitories should therefore include provisions on minimum quality requirements (e.g. number of residents per room, number of bathrooms, etc.) and provide increased statutory protection for residents.

Adopt a metropolitan-area approach to housing (including social housing), transport and spatial planning

Housing and land use planning policies should be co-ordinated at the level of the FUA. Municipalities within the Czech Republic are very small by international standards. This limits the administrative capacity of municipalities and increases the need for co-ordination across municipal boundaries. While a wide range of tools for intermunicipal co-operation exists in the Czech Republic, few concern the housing sector.

Developing joint housing, transport and spatial plans at the metropolitan level can help overcome the consequences of administrative fragmentation and steer housing development to locations that are well connected to public transport and close to employment centres. The national government should continue to support intermunicipal co-operation and joint service provision, including by providing financial incentives for it.

Leverage fiscal and financial instruments more effectively to support housing affordability

Due to their low level of fiscal autonomy, Czech municipalities tend to compete with one another to attract the population and increase their share of government transfers. As indicated in several OECD reports (Blöchliger, 2015[16]; OECD, 2020[17]), the Czech Republic is not using property tax to its full advantage. At 0.6% of total government tax revenue in 2018, the recurrent tax on immovable property is very low compared to the OECD average of 3.1%. The same holds true for the subnational level: property tax on land and buildings accounts for 4.3% of subnational government tax revenue, 2% of total consolidated subnational government revenue and 0.2% of GDP, which is well below the OECD average of 1.1% of GDP. The base rate is set centrally and municipalities can raise the rate to five times the minimum threshold amount. However, most municipalities tend to set their local property tax rate at the lowest level. Only 7% of municipalities have made use of the possibility to increase tax rates (Janouskova and Sobotovicova, 2016[18]). If more municipalities used their power to increase property tax rates, this could directly augment municipalities' tax revenue, thus enabling them to invest more money in housing. To avoid resistance from municipalities to the tax and unintended consequences (e.g. in terms of increasing the housing burden for low-income households), targeted means-tested exemptions could be introduced, such as exemptions for low-income households.

A differentiated property tax could also be used to incentivise more efficient land use through higher-density housing development, discourage low-density housing and promote brownfield developments. Such instruments are currently underused by Czech municipalities and constitute a missed opportunity. In particular, property tax does not capture changes in market value as the calculation of the tax is based on the size of property rather than its value. The tax evaluation should be based on regularly updated estimates of property value rather than size, as is currently the case. Rather than allowing private individuals and businesses to retain the entire market value benefit from increased property values attributable to public spending and investment, municipalities in the Czech Republic could take steps to "capture" a portion of the increases in value. A shift to a value-based property tax and/or the implementation of various "value-capture" mechanisms linked to specific public infrastructure projects would help achieve such an objective.

In addition to residential developments, commercial and industrial developments often occur on greenspace. Complicating the issue of new development are the many old industrial or brownfield sites in the Czech Republic. Even though these sites represent potential development sites and their redevelopment should be encouraged, they can be very difficult to revitalise. The remediation required by brownfield sites poses an obstacle to their use as municipalities may lack the funds that would be necessary for their rehabilitation. In order to use brownfield sites while encouraging the development of affordable housing, programmes giving tax breaks or subsidies to developers for land remediation in return for the provision of affordable housing could be considered.

Czech local and national governments could tap into current and upcoming sources of financing, such as those offered by the EU in the context of the recovery package and the Renovation Wave,[1] and especially the Affordable Housing Initiative (AHI).[2] This initiative will provide support, knowledge and expertise to local industrial partnerships with the ambition to pilot lighthouse renovation neighbourhoods, putting liveability, sustainability and socially responsible business models at the forefront. Given the labour-intensive nature of the building sector, improving the existing housing stock, including in terms of energy efficiency, could also foster post-COVID-19 recovery in the Czech Republic.

Action plan

Recommendation 1

Steer housing development to urban areas with high housing demand

In order to increase affordable housing supply in urban areas where it is most needed and prevent sprawl and vacant housing in areas where demand for housing is low, housing development needs to target urban areas where housing demand is high.

Actions

- Provide clear national and regional guidance to local planning policies.
- Use local land-planning instruments to encourage private-sector construction of affordable housing.
- Ensure compact, transport-oriented development to reduce auxiliary costs of housing in cities.
- Manage publicly owned land strategically and use it for the provision of affordable housing where possible.
- Monitor the effectiveness of the reform of the building permit process.

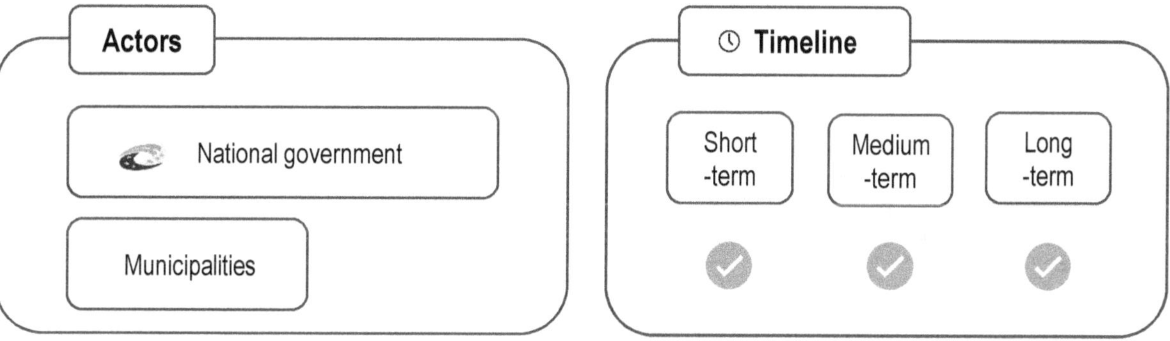

Recommendation 2

Provide more alternatives to homeownership

With house prices increasing more rapidly than incomes, especially in cities, homeownership has become inaccessible for most newcomers to the housing market. Supply of alternative housing for low-income and middle-income households needs to increase.

Actions

- Encourage municipalities to give equal weight to rental housing in their planning policies.
- Introduce a national deposit scheme and rent guarantees to support vulnerable households access the rental market and reduce risks of rent loss for landlords to increase rental (including social) housing supply.
- Reform housing co-operatives.
- Involve non-governmental actors in the provision of affordable housing.

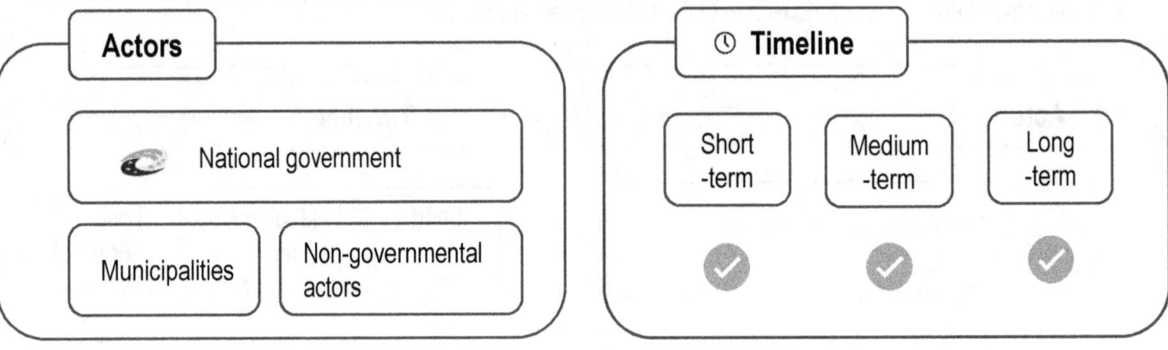

Recommendation 3

Increase the supply of social housing

The social housing stock in the Czech Republic is too small to meet the demand of all low-income and vulnerable households. Furthermore, social housing in the Czech Republic is mostly provided by municipalities, which have complete autonomy in deciding how to use the housing stock that they own, which can create a lack of transparency in the social housing system.

Actions

- Increase public investment in social housing.
- Introduce a national social housing policy framework that guides municipal social housing.
- Remove barriers to access social housing by exploring other options such as allowing municipalities to withhold rent payments from the housing allowance in case of repeated failure to pay rent.

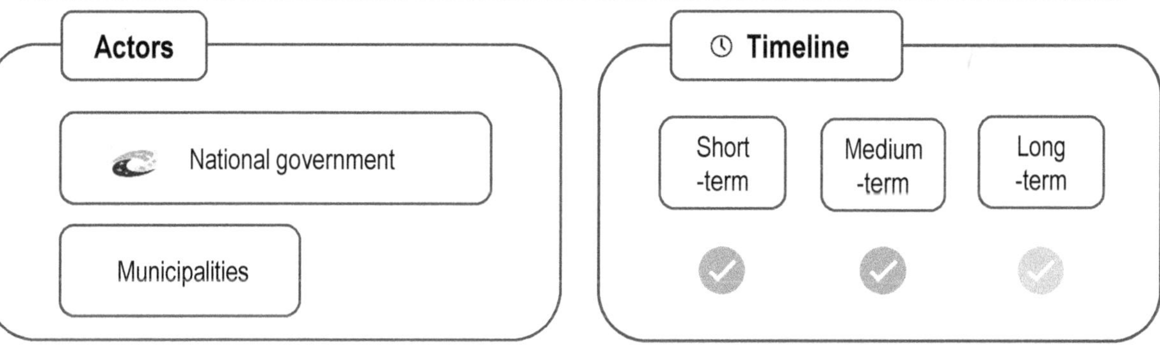

Recommendation 4

Ensure the most vulnerable people have access to adequate housing

As private rental accommodations leased at market rate have become financially inaccessible for many Czech households and availability of municipal social housing is limited, many households have no choice but to turn to alternative housing with substandard conditions, such as dormitories. Furthermore, many Czech households eligible for the housing allowance or supplement do not access the benefits available to them.

Actions

- Simplify the application process for housing allowances and subsidies, and ensure it remains accessible to those who need them the most.
- Strengthen the regulation of dormitories to protect residents.

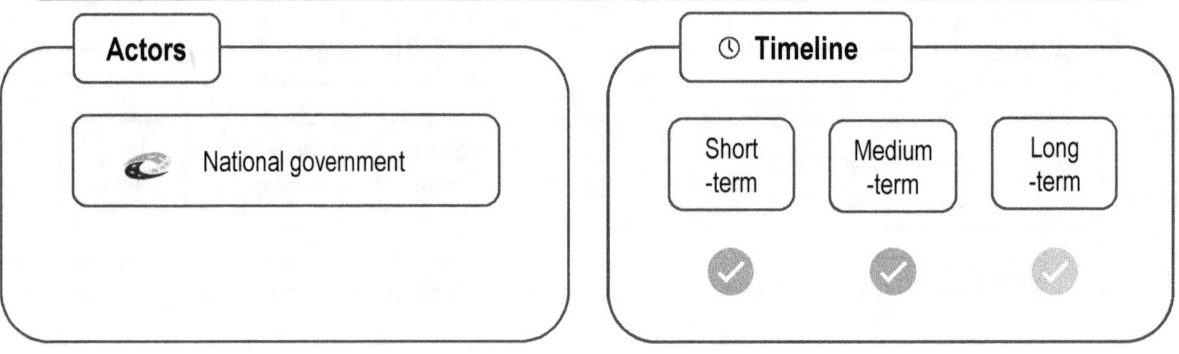

Recommendation 5

Adopt a metropolitan approach to housing (including social housing), transport and spatial planning

Municipalities within the Czech Republic are very small by international standards. This limits the administrative capacity of municipalities and increases the need for co-ordination across municipal boundaries. While a wide range of tools for intermunicipal co-operation exist in the country, few concern the housing sector.

Actions

- Develop joint housing, transport and spatial plans at the metropolitan level.
- Continue to support intermunicipal co-operation and joint service provision, including by providing financial incentives for it.

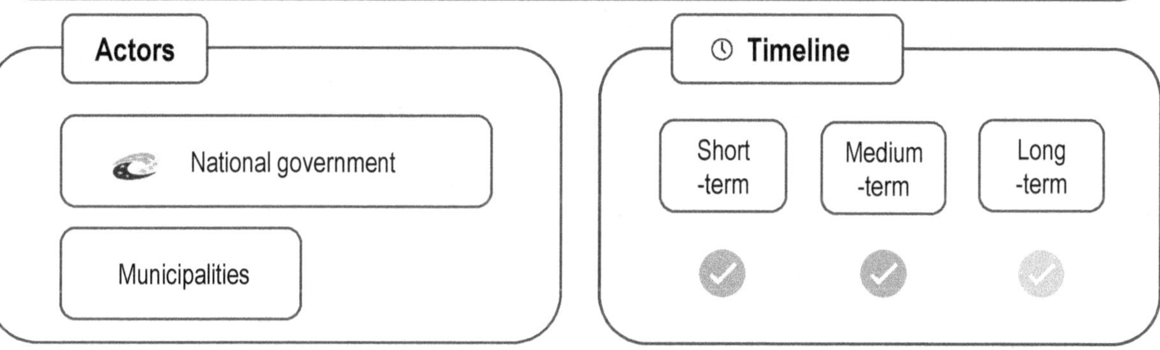

Recommendation 6

Leverage fiscal and financial instruments more effectively to support housing affordability

The subnational government finance structure of the Czech Republic leaves little autonomy for municipalities. However, fiscal instruments can be leveraged at the local and national levels to increase revenues for affordable housing development and to steer housing developments towards the desired locations.

Actions

- Encourage municipalities to make use of their power to increase property tax rates, while introducing targeted means-tested exemptions.
- Base property tax evaluation on regularly updated estimates of property value rather than size.
- Institute "value-capture" mechanisms linked to specific public infrastructure projects.
- Encourage the use of brownfield sites for the development of affordable housing by giving tax breaks or subsidies to developers for land remediation in return for the provision of affordable housing.
- Tap into current and upcoming external sources of financing such as those from the European Union, in particular to improve the existing stock of housing.

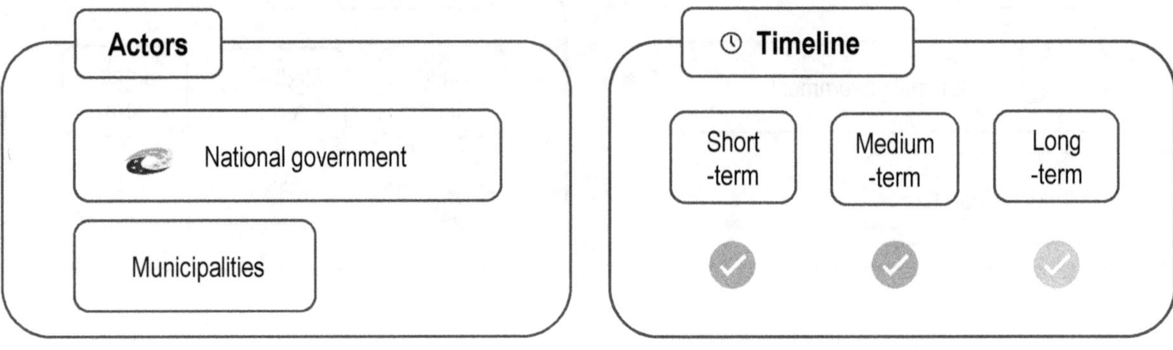

Recommendations for the City of Pilsen (Plzeň)

Use instruments at the municipal level to increase housing affordability

The city of Pilsen is struggling with high house prices that are limiting access to the housing market for many households, especially the most vulnerable ones. In order to increase its supply of affordable housing, the city of Pilsen could use both direct and indirect instruments.

Actions

- Use the possibility of increasing property tax rates when relevant and introduce targeted means-tested exemptions to increase municipal revenue to invest in social and affordable housing.
- Evaluate the ratio of municipally owned "normal" housing units to social housing units and consider moving some housing units from the former to the latter.
- Review social housing eligibility requirements to facilitate access in particular to the "chronically" homeless population and to foreigners, in order to decrease the number of dormitory residents in sub-standard conditions.
- Leverage local land use planning and zoning instruments more to encourage private-sector construction of affordable housing in desired locations.
- Broaden the use of developer obligations within local land use planning policies such as inclusionary zoning (i.e. the requirement on developers to provide a share of housing units in new developments as affordable rental units).
- Co-ordinate land use planning and housing strategies with surrounding municipalities.

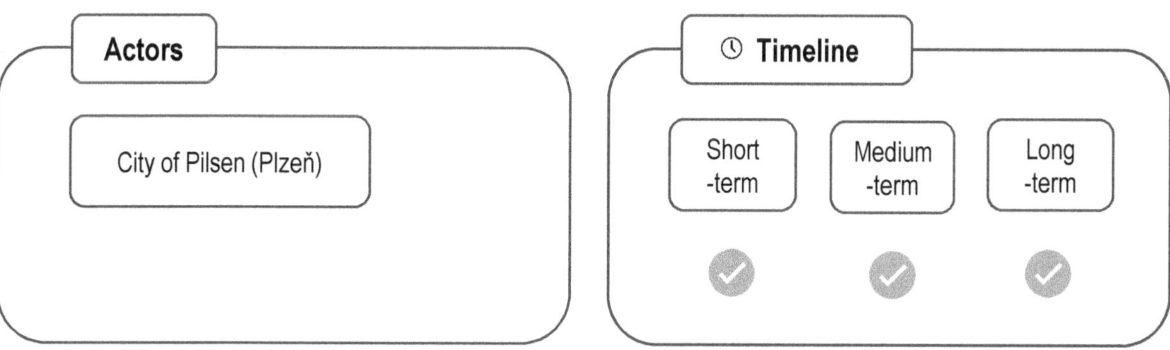

Recommendations for the City of Olomouc

Use instruments at the municipal level to increase housing affordability

The city of Olomouc has experienced a strong increase in house prices in the past couple of decades, partly driven by a large population of students and teachers from Palacký University. In order to increase its supply of affordable housing, the city of Olomouc could use both direct and indirect instruments.

Actions

- Use the possibility of increasing property tax rates when relevant and introduce targeted means-tested exemptions to increase municipal revenue to invest in social and affordable housing.
- Evaluate the balance between different types of municipally owned housing and, if possible, move housing units from the regular municipally owned housing stock to the social housing stock.
- Use municipally owned land to build affordable housing and conclude joint development agreements with private developers.
- Make criteria for choosing successful applicants for the regular municipal housing stock more transparent and increase access to social housing for dormitory residents.
- Implement short-term solutions for vulnerable households, including creating family shelters, while working to facilitate access to private rental housing.
- Further leverage local land use planning and zoning instruments to encourage private sector construction of affordable housing in desired locations.
- Broaden the use of developer obligations within local land use planning policies such as inclusionary zoning (i.e. the requirement for developers to provide a share of housing units in new developments as affordable rental units).
- Co-ordinate land use planning and housing strategies with surrounding municipalities.

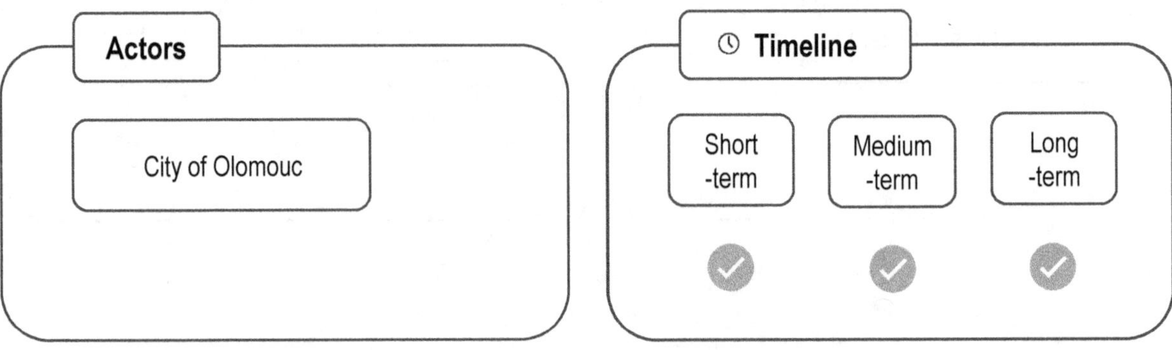

References

Blöchliger, H. (2015), "Reforming the Tax on Immovable Property: Taking Care of the Unloved", *OECD Economics Department Working Papers*, No. 1205, OECD Publishing, Paris, https://doi.org/10.1787/5js30tw0n7kg-en. [16]

CNB (2020), *Financial Stability Report 2019/2020*, Czech National Bank, https://www.cnb.cz/export/sites/cnb/en/financial-stability/.galleries/fs_reports/fsr_2019-2020/fsr_2019-2020.pdf. [3]

de Boer, R. and R. Bitetti (2014), "A Revival of the Private Rental Sector of the Housing Market?: Lessons from Germany, Finland, the Czech Republic and the Netherlands", *OECD Economics Department Working Papers*, No. 1170, OECD Publishing, Paris, https://dx.doi.org/10.1787/5jxv9f32j0zp-en. [9]

Deloitte (2020), *Property Index: Overview of European Residential Markets.* [4]

Dijkstra, L., H. Poelman and P. Veneri (2019), "The EU-OECD definition of a functional urban area", *OECD Regional Development Working Papers*, No. 2019/11, OECD Publishing, Paris, https://dx.doi.org/10.1787/d58cb34d-en. [15]

EU Urban Agenda Housing Partnership (2017), *EU Urban Agenda-Housing Partnership Guidance Paper on EU Regulation & Public Support for Housing*, https://ec.europa.eu/futurium/sites/futurium/files/housing_partnership_-_guidance_paper_on_eu_regulation_and_public_support_for_housing_03-2017.pdf. [14]

European Commission (2020), *COMMUNICATION FROM THE COMMISSION TO THE EUROPEAN PARLIAMENT, THE COUNCIL, THE EUROPEAN ECONOMIC AND SOCIAL COMMITTEE AND THE COMMITTEE OF THE REGIONS: A Renovation Wave for Europe - greening our buildings, creating jobs, improving lives*, https://ec.europa.eu/energy/sites/ener/files/eu_renovation_wave_strategy.pdf. [19]

Guerra, E. and M. Kirschen (2016), "Housing Plus Transportation Affordability Indices: Uses, Opportunities, and Challenges", *International Transport Forum Discussion Papers*, No. 2016/14, OECD Publishing, Paris, https://dx.doi.org/10.1787/a1fc9b79-en. [13]

Janouskova, J. and Š. Sobotovicova (2016), "Immovable property tax in the Czech Republic as an instrument of fiscal decentralization", *Technological and Economic Development of Economy*, Vol. 22/6, pp. 767-782, http://dx.doi.org/10.3846/20294913.2016.1236355. [18]

Litman, T. (2016), *Transportation Cost and Benefit Analysis (second edition)*, Victoria Transport Policy Institute. [11]

Ministry of Regional Development (2011), *Housing Policy Concept of the Czech Republic Till 2020*, State Housing Development Fund, Ministry of Regional Development of the Czech Republic, https://www.bmszki.hu/sites/default/files/fajlok/node-293/housing_policy_concept_till_2020.pdf. [8]

OECD (2020), *Affordable Housing Database*, OECD, Paris, http://oe.cd/ahd. [2]

OECD (2020), *OECD Economic Surveys: Czech Republic 2020*, OECD Publishing, Paris, https://doi.org/10.1787/1b180a5a-en (accessed on 29 January 2021). [17]

OECD (2017), *The Governance of Land Use in the Czech Republic: The Case of Prague*, OECD Publishing, Paris, https://doi.org/10.1787/9789264281936-en. [10]

OECD (forthcoming), *Housing Synthesis Report*, OECD Publishing, Paris. [1]

OECD/EC (2020), *Cities in the World: A New Perspective on Urbanisation*, OECD Urban Studies, OECD Publishing, Paris, https://dx.doi.org/10.1787/d0efcbda-en. [5]

Office of the Government (2019), *2019 European Semester: National Reform Programme of the Czech Republic 2019*, https://ec.europa.eu/info/sites/info/files/2019-european-semester-national-reform-programme-czech-republic_en.pdf. [7]

Shoup, D. (2005), *The High Cost of Free Parking*, American Planning Association. [12]

World Bank (2019), *Doing Business 2020*, World Bank, Washington, DC. [6]

Notes

[1] COM (2020)662 final of 14 October 2020 (European Commission, 2020[19]).

[2] See page 22 of COM (2020)662 final of 14 October 2020 (European Commission, 2020[19]).

1 Overview of housing affordability in cities in the Czech Republic

House prices in the Czech Republic have soared faster than household disposable income, especially in cities where house prices have often risen at a faster pace than the national average. While the rise in house prices may benefit the large share of Czech homeowners, it has made it even harder for newcomers, especially the young, to get a foot on the housing ladder. With rents also rising and with relatively limited supply, the private rental market offers few alternatives for people struggling to find affordable housing. Many low- and middle-income households are therefore getting priced out of cities, or have no choice but to turn to substandard quality housing. While structural drivers pushing housing demand up in Czech cities are likely to remain despite the COVID-19 crisis, housing development does not happen where it is most needed, i.e. where demand for housing is highest, driving house prices up in Czech cities. Furthermore, Czech households bear a heavy financial burden by living in cities where the housing stock is often old and in need of energy efficiency improvements.

Introduction

As in many other OECD countries, many households in the Czech Republic are increasingly struggling to access a decent, affordable home, with house prices reaching new highs and incomes falling out of pace. This is especially the case for low-income households or households at risk of poverty, elderly people and single-parent families. The challenge of housing affordability is even more acute in cities and urban areas, where property and rental prices have often increased faster than in the Czech Republic in general and housing cost overburden and overcrowding rates are higher.

At the time of writing this report, the COVID-19 pandemic has been unfolding around the world and continues to shake housing markets. While the long-term impacts of the pandemic on the housing market in the Czech Republic remain uncertain, the crisis has brought to the fore many of the longstanding issues the Czech Republic was facing, such as housing insecurity, homelessness and housing inequalities.

After briefly defining housing affordability, this chapter starts with an overview of the historical context and the influence it had on the Czech Republic's housing market. It then focuses on housing affordability in Czech cities by exploring the evolution of house prices and the main drivers for both demand and supply, examining the burden of total housing-related costs that Czech households need to shoulder and assessing the quality of housing in Czech cities, including housing's energy efficiency, in comparison with the rest of the country and other OECD countries.

To support the analysis, the OECD, in co-operation with the Ministry of Regional Development of the Czech Republic (MMR), carried out a survey on 1 877 Czech municipalities in August/September 2020 to collect data on the housing market and housing policies at the municipal level. The survey will hereinafter be referred to as the "OECD-MMR housing survey". The survey covered all municipalities within functional urban areas (FUAs) of more than 50 000 inhabitants as defined by the OECD,[1] as well as the municipalities within the FUAs of Jablonec and Mladá Boleslav (see Annex A for further details on the administration of the survey). Results from this survey are included in the chapters of the report.

Defining housing affordability

In the absence of a universally agreed definition of housing affordability, several organisations and countries measure housing affordability in different ways, ranging from price-to-income and housing expenditure-to-income ratios to housing quality measures (Box 1.1).

At its core, housing affordability is linked to the ability of households to pay for a dwelling. Housing affordability is therefore often seen as a function of housing costs and the income of the household. Housing costs are, in turn, driven by several factors including house prices, rents, mortgages, but also insurance, mandatory services and charges (e.g. sewage and refuse removal charges), regular maintenance and repairs, taxes and the cost of utilities (water, electricity, gas and heating). However, affordability is not only about housing costs per se. It also involves the location of housing, the access that housing provides to jobs and economic opportunities, public goods and services, as well as its quality:

- Housing location is an important component of housing affordability, as poor housing location can make seemingly affordable housing unaffordable for low-income families. When households live in isolated and remote areas, where housing is cheaper, they tend to spend more on transport and commute for longer hours, making housing more expensive and decreasing their well-being.
- Furthermore, living in cheaper but less well-connected areas can reduce access to public services (education, health, etc.), to public space (pavements, streets, public parks, commercial areas, etc.) and jobs and economic opportunities.

- It is also critical to take into account the quality of housing. Beyond the walls and roof sheltering people, housing is a place where people should feel safe, have enough physical space and enjoy adequate sanitary conditions. Whether the dwelling responds to the household's specific needs also determines its quality, e.g. its accessibility for elderly people or people with disabilities. Energy efficiency is at the intersection of housing quality and financial affordability, as energy-efficient and better-insulated homes reduce the risk of dampness and provide warmer homes, thus improving living conditions while reducing energy bills and improving housing affordability. Considering that low-income households tend to spend relatively more on heating their homes than higher-income households, improving energy efficiency in housing constitutes a key factor to build more inclusive housing markets.

Box 1.1. Selection of definitions and measures of housing affordability

UN-Habitat states that "The underlying principle [of housing affordability] is that household financial costs associated with housing should not threaten or compromise the attainment and satisfaction of other basic needs such as food, education, access to health care, transport, etc. Based on the existing method and data of UN-Habitat's Urban Indicators Program (1996-2006), unaffordability is currently measured as the **net monthly expenditure on housing cost that exceeds 30% of the total monthly income of the household**" (UN, 2018[1]).

In 2010, a **European Commission** communication (the "European platform against poverty and social exclusion: a European framework for social and territorial cohesion") addressed the issue of affordable accommodation by declaring that "access to affordable accommodation is a fundamental need and right" (European Commission, 2010[2]). In Europe, housing affordability is analysed through **the housing cost overburden rate** which is the share of the population in a country living in households that spend 40% or more of their disposable income on housing (Eurostat, n.d.[3]).

Country examples

The **Australian Bureau of Statistics** measures housing affordability as the **ratio of housing costs to gross household income**.

In **the United Kingdom**, the Office for National Statistics calculates a **housing affordability ratio** by dividing house prices by annual earnings, with data for new dwellings, existing dwellings and all dwellings combined, while earnings are available on a workplace basis and a place of residence basis (Office for National Statistics, 2020[4]).

The United States Federal Reserve defines the issue of housing affordability by the **rate of the housing cost burden**, i.e. the share of households that spend more than 30% of their income on housing costs (Dumont, 2019[5]).

Various **housing quality measures** are also used to assess housing affordability, such as the number of rooms per person, the overcrowding rate and the housing deprivation rate. Canada's statistical office **Statistics Canada**, for example, defines **suitable housing** as housing with enough bedrooms for the size and composition of the household.

Source: UN (2018[1]), "Metadata Indicator 11.1.1: Proportion of urban population living in slums, informal settlements or inadequate housing", https://unstats.un.org/sdgs/metadata/files/Metadata-11-01-01.pdf; Eurostat (n.d.[3]), *Housing Statistics: Statistics Explained*; Office for National Statistics (2020[4]), *Housing Affordability in England and Wales: 2019*; Dumont, A. (2019[5]), *Housing Affordability in the US: Trends by Geography, Tenure, and Household Income*, https://doi.org/10.17016/2380-7172.2430.

Accommodation can therefore be considered affordable if: i) households can afford to buy *or* rent it; ii) households can afford to live in it (i.e. living in the accommodation does not overburden the households' finances, when taking into account operation and maintenance costs as well as utility expenses, so that they are able to pay for other obligations); and iii) it is adequate (i.e. it is of good quality and meets the needs of its occupants). This definition will be used hereinafter to assess and analyse housing affordability in cities in the Czech Republic.

The Czech housing market has a historically owner-dominated structure

As in many other former communist countries in Central and Eastern Europe, homeownership is the dominant type of tenure in the Czech Republic, with 75% of households owning their accommodation (i.e. 59% of households live in a dwelling that is owned outright and 16% in a dwelling that is owned with an outstanding mortgage or housing loan). The rate of homeownership is also high amongst low-income households, with 58% of households in the bottom quintile of the income distribution owning their dwelling outright in 2018, i.e. without an outstanding mortgage or housing loan. While the share of outright owners in the Czech Republic is well above the OECD average of around 43%, it is lower than in other former socialist countries. In Lithuania, the Slovak Republic or Hungary, for example, outright homeownership accounts for 80%, 76% and 73% of households respectively. This is mirrored by a relatively important role played by the private rental market in the Czech Republic compared with other countries in Central and Eastern Europe. Almost 18% of Czech households rent their dwelling from the private rental sector, which is lower than the average in OECD countries (25%) but remains higher than in many other former socialist countries. The share of households that rent their dwelling from the subsidised market (state-owned or other) is very low, at 1.4% of all households (OECD, 2020[6]) (Figure 1.1).

Figure 1.1. Housing tenure distribution in OECD countries, 2018 or latest year available

Share of households in different types of tenure, in percentage

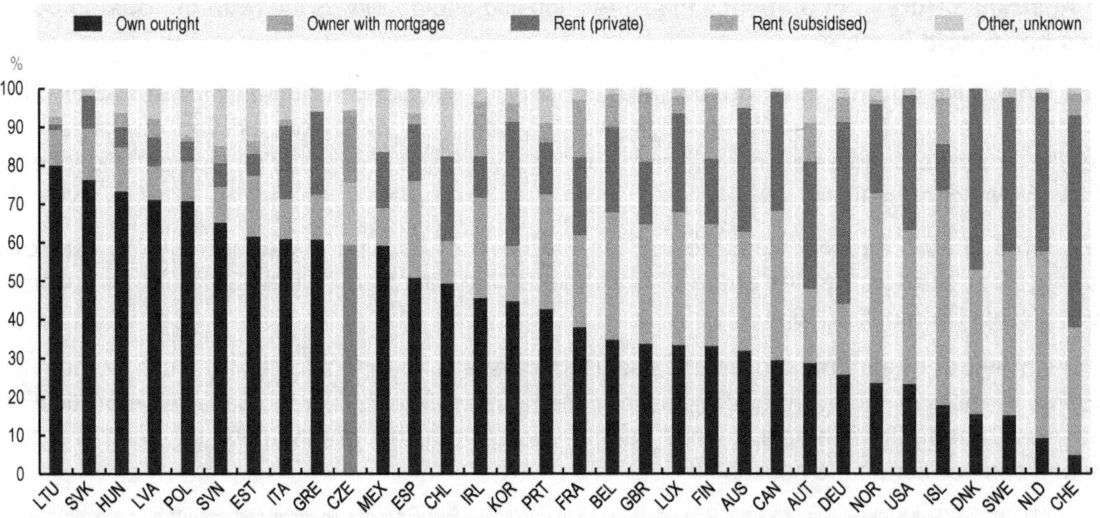

Note: Tenants renting at subsidised rent are grouped together with tenants renting at private rent in Australia, Canada, Chile, Denmark, Mexico, the Netherlands and the United States, and are not capturing the full extent of coverage in Sweden due to data limitations.
Source: OECD (2020[6]), *Affordable Housing Database*, http://oe.cd/ahd.

The housing tenure distribution in the Czech Republic, and especially the prevalence of homeownership and the relative importance of the private rental market, results from the transition to a market economy since 1989 and the subsequent privatisation of the housing stock. During the communist regime, which started in 1948, the Czech economy was governed by central planning and most of the economy was state-owned, including the housing stock. Almost all private multi-unit buildings that had been built during the construction boom between 1920 and 1938 or earlier were expropriated to become state property, with landlords forced to sell their property to the state at very low prices. State rental housing, therefore, became the dominant tenure in city centres, with the government allocating state-owned flats according to people's needs and at a very low rent (Lux and Sunega, 2010[7]). Tenants who were allotted flats by the state obtained unlimited occupancy rights and tenants were able to transfer their "right of use" to their relatives or to exchange it with other user right holders (Lux and Mikeszova, 2012[8]).

After the Velvet Revolution of 1989 and the change of regime, privatisation of the housing stock occurred via two main channels: i) through the restitution of the public housing stock that had been expropriated between 1948 and 1989, which was returned to their previous owners or their descendants by restitution laws; and ii) through the sale of the dwellings to sitting tenants at below-market prices, as low as 5% to 10% of the actual value (de Boer and Bitetti, 2014[9]). By 1993, most of the property transfers to private owners had been completed (about 6%-7% of the whole Czech housing stock) (Lux and Mikeszova, 2012[8]), mainly in towns and cities. In central Prague, for example, around 70% of all houses were returned to their previous owners.

This process of transition from a socialist to a market economy has had a deep and lasting impact on the structure of the Czech housing market. In 1991, homeownership constituted 38% of the housing stock, 9% for co-operative housing and 39% for public rental, while private renting was almost non-existent (de Boer and Bitetti, 2014[9]). By 2018, homeownership and private renting had jumped to 75% and 18% respectively, while only 1.4% of Czech households rented their accommodation through the public subsidised rental market.

The very small size of the municipality-owned housing market, including social housing rented out at below-market rates, also finds its roots in the historical context. The municipal rental sector was created after 1991 with the transfer of around 1.44 million state-owned dwellings to municipalities, i.e. about 39% of the housing stock in the Czech Republic. Municipalities became free to manage and allocate public housing, with no state regulatory framework, regulations on public housing allocation or requirements to provide housing to poor and vulnerable households. Faced with rent regulation preventing them from introducing any effective way of managing their housing stock without subsidising it and a lack of financial and human resources to ensure the maintenance of it, many municipalities privatised a major part of their housing stock (Lux and Sunega, 2017[10]). Today, social rental dwellings account for only 0.4% of the total number of dwellings in the Czech Republic – a very low share compared with other OECD countries (e.g. 37.8% in the Netherlands, 20% in Austria, 7.6% in Poland and 4.0% in Hungary (OECD, 2020[6])).

The privatisation of the housing stock also gave rise to the emergence of a private rental sector that used to be virtually non-existent prior to the transition from communism. While the private rental sector plays a relatively important role in the Czech housing market and has experienced stronger growth than in most other central and eastern European countries, a split market has hampered the development of the private rental market into a strong and stable tenancy (de Boer and Bitetti, 2014[9]). The market was indeed split between existing contracts of sitting tenants, whose occupancy rights remained unaltered by the restitution of the flats to their original owners, and new contracts for which free market rental prices could be charged from 1993 to promote investments in rental housing. This created a divide between the "privileged" historical tenants – who had rent thresholds set by national governments and tenure security – and the "non-privileged" new tenants – whose rents fell under a liberal system of no regulation on rent setting or lease term and who had no effective tenant protection (Lux and Mikeszova, 2012[8]). In 2007, rents for sitting tenants started to adjust gradually to market rents, reducing the divide between regulated rents and free market rents. The deregulation was completed by 2012 and has helped create a more competitive private rental market, increase private rental supply and improve accessibility for outsiders. However, deregulation has also led to a significant decrease in rent setting protection for tenants and altered the demand on the market, with private renting being seen as a temporary housing option for Czech households, even among young people (Lux and Sunega, 2010[7]).

Many Czech households are struggling to access affordable housing, especially in cities

House prices in the Czech Republic have increased sharply over the past few years, much faster than household incomes, particularly in cities. While the rise in house prices is not necessarily an issue for the large share of Czech households that already own their dwelling and do not plan to move, purchasing new housing remains out of reach for most newcomers to the housing market. As rents have also been increasing, the private rental market offers few alternative housing options.

House prices in the Czech Republic have increased faster than incomes

Since reaching their post-financial crisis low in 2013, house prices in the Czech Republic have increased sharply and now largely exceed their pre-crisis level. Between the first quarter of 2013 and the second quarter of 2020, real house prices rose by 43.1% – a much higher growth rate than in the OECD, where real house prices increased by 24.9% on average over the same period (Figure 1.2). In 2018 alone, house prices increased by 7.1% in the Czech Republic – the fourth highest annual growth rate among all OECD countries, just under the growth rates observed in Hungary, Latvia and Portugal. While the pace of house price increase has slowed down since 2018, house prices still rose by 6.3% between the fourth quarter (Q4) of 2018 and Q4 2019 – much more than in the euro area on average (3.8%) and more than twice as fast as in the OECD on average (2.5%). Estimates from the Czech National Bank (CNB) indicate that the Czech housing market has been overvalued since 2017 and was overvalued by around 25% at the end of 2019 (CNB, 2020[11]).

Figure 1.2. Real house prices, change between Q1 2013 and Q2 2020

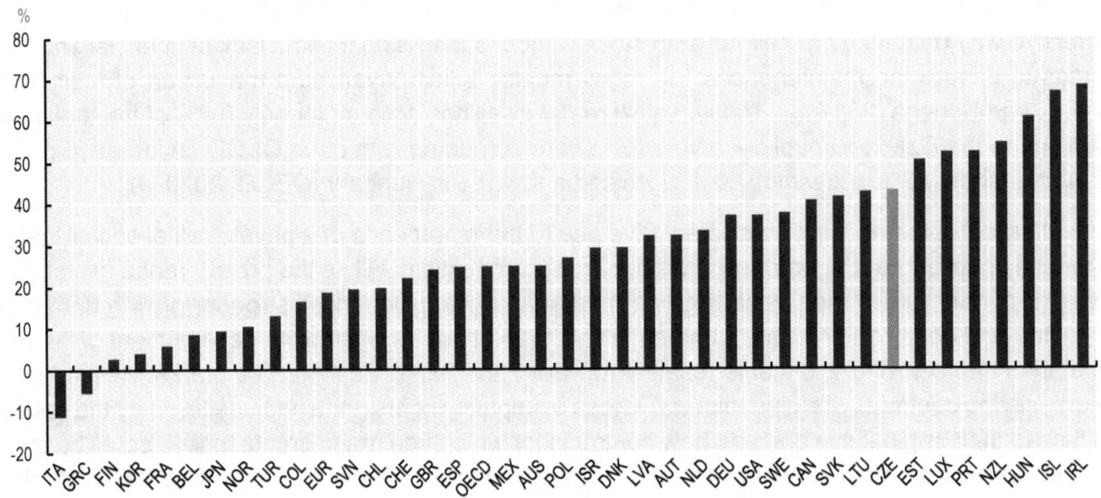

Note: Real house prices are nominal house prices deflated using the private consumption deflator from the national account statistics. Data for New Zealand show the change in real house prices between Q1 2013 and Q1 2020.
Source: OECD (2021[12]), *Analytical House Price Indicators Database*, https://stats.oecd.org/.

House prices in the Czech Republic have soared faster than household disposable income, making housing increasingly unaffordable for first-time buyers, renters and those who have to move from cheap areas into more expensive ones for work reasons for example. Since 2015, the price-to-income ratio in the Czech Republic has experienced one of the fastest increases among all OECD countries (Figure 1.3). Real house prices have steadily outpaced real wage growth – at an average rate of 2.6 percentage points per year since 2013 – which has undermined housing affordability even in the context of declining borrowing costs (EC, 2020[13]).

While the rise in house prices may benefit the large share of Czech households that own their dwelling (due to the rise in the value of their assets), it means that purchasing new housing remains out of reach for most newcomers to the housing market. This may in turn hinder upward social mobility, as current and future generations are less able to purchase property than their parents (OECD, 2019[14]). Currently, Czech households need to save more than 11 years of gross annual salaries to buy a standardised new dwelling of 70 square metres (m²), compared to about 9 years in Latvia, and about 7 years in Hungary and Poland (Deloitte, 2020[15]).

Figure 1.3. Price-to-income ratio, Q2 2020 or latest available

Index, 2015=100

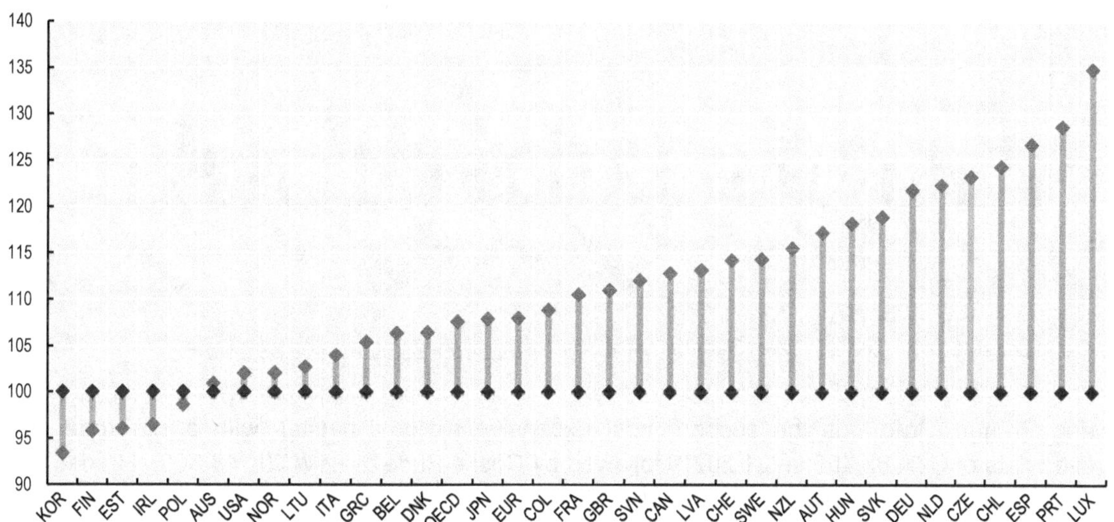

Note: Nominal house prices divided by nominal disposable income per head.
Source: OECD (2021[12]), *Analytical House Price Indicators Database*, https://stats.oecd.org/.

House prices are particularly high in Czech cities, aggravating the housing affordability crisis for urban residents

While house price growth has varied considerably across regions, it has generally been higher in cities than in the rest of the Czech Republic. Across the Czech Republic, the larger the municipalities are in terms of population, the more expensive housing is, suggesting that there is a price premium for living in cities. In all 13 regions of the Czech Republic, house prices are consistently higher in municipalities that have more than 50 000 inhabitants than in municipalities with fewer inhabitants (Figure 1.4).

Prague is the most expensive city in the Czech Republic. In the first quarter of 2020, the average price of purchased flats in Prague was CZK 88 100 (EUR 3 340) per m², reaching as much as CZK 159 800 (EUR 6 060) per m² in district Prague 1 (1 of the 22 administrative districts of Prague which includes most of the medieval centre of the city). This was almost 50% higher than the average price of purchased flats in all regional capitals of the Czech Republic at CZK 65 400 (EUR 2 480). According to the Czech Statistical Office, Prague also recorded the strongest price growth (41.7%) since 2010 for all types of real estate among all regions in the Czech Republic (Czech Statistical Office, 2020[16]). Purchasing prices for new flats in Prague increased by 64% since 2010 and by 10.7% between the first quarter of 2019 and the first quarter of 2020. According to the Eurostat perception survey, as many as 70% of inhabitants of the FUA of Prague either strongly disagreed or somewhat disagreed that it was easy to find good housing at a reasonable price in 2019, compared with about 35% of the population of Ostrava.

Figure 1.4. Flat prices by region and by population size of municipalities in the Czech Republic

Average purchase price of flats in the 13 regions of the Czech Republic and Prague, by size of municipalities, 2016-18

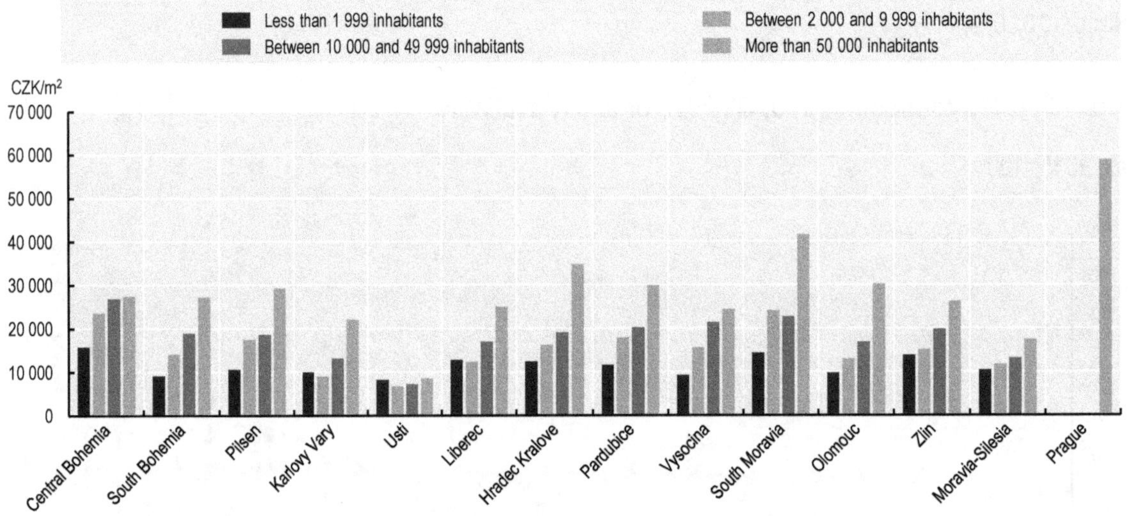

Source: Czech Statistical Office (2020[16]), *Czech Statistical Office Statistics*, https://www.czso.cz/csu/czso/statistics.

Following Prague, Brno was the second most expensive regional capital, with an average price of purchased flats of CZK 65 400 in Q1 2020, followed by Ceske Budejovice (CZK 48 800), Hradec Kralove (CZK 44 900) and Pilsen (CZK 44 700) (Deloitte, 2020[17]).

Rent prices have increased steadily but at a slower pace than house purchase prices

The private rental sector provides a housing option to the segments of the population who cannot afford to enter the homeownership market or do not have access to the social housing market, due to ineligibility or inefficiencies such as long waiting lists. While homeownership remains the preferred tenure for Czech households, a fast increase in house prices combined with caps on mortgage loans (nine times borrowers' net annual incomes since 2018) has hampered access to homeownership for newcomers, pushing more households towards other types of tenures.

Even though the private rental sector has expanded since the 1990s, it only accounts for around 13%-14% of the total housing stock. However, this national average masks territorial variations within the Czech Republic, as cities tend to have a higher stock of private rental housing than the rest of the country. In Prague, for example, about one-third of the housing stock is rented.

Rent prices in major cities are higher than in the rest of the Czech Republic. In 2019, the average monthly rent in Prague was EUR 12.3 per m², which means that a tenant pays on average EUR 740 a month for a 60-m² flat (Deloitte, 2020[15]). While this remains lower than rent prices in large European metropolitan areas such as Amsterdam, London and Paris, rent prices in Prague are similar to those in other major cities in Europe such as Marseille (France), Milan (Italy) and Rotterdam (Netherlands). They are also higher than in Lisbon (Portugal), Vienna (Austria) and Berlin (Germany), where the average monthly rents were EUR 11.8, EUR 9.9 and EUR 9.1 per m² respectively. In Brno and Ostrava, the average rent prices were EUR 9.6 and EUR 6.4 per m² respectively (Figure 1.5).

Figure 1.5. Rental prices in selected countries and European cities

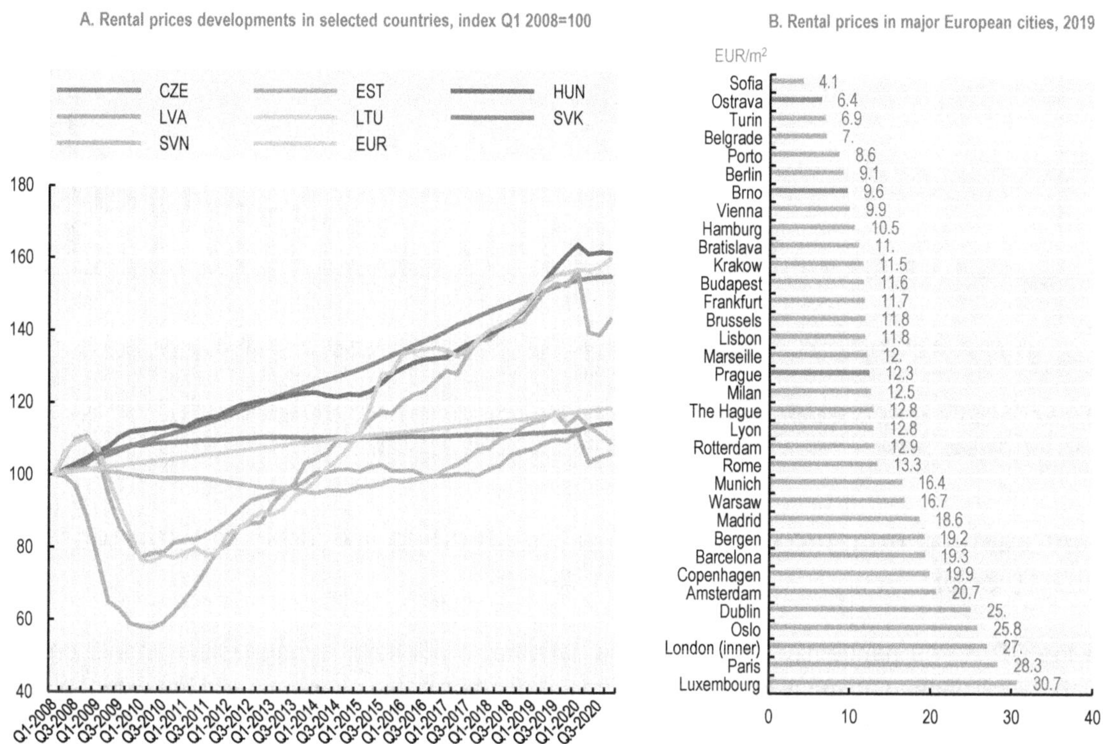

Sources OECD (2021[12]), *Analytical House Price Indicators Database*, https://stats.oecd.org/; Deloitte (2020[15]), *Property Index: Overview of European Residential Markets*.

Since 2005, real rent prices have almost doubled in the Czech Republic – one of the largest increases among OECD countries (Figure 1.6). Although much of the rise in rents since 2005 can be explained by rent deregulation and catch-up from low rent levels inherited from the socialist regime, the increase has also been strong in more recent years – and stronger than in some neighbouring countries (Figure 1.5).

However, the rise in rents has not been as strong as the rise in house purchase prices. Between the second quarter of 2019 and the second quarter of 2020, rent prices in the Czech Republic increased by 3.7%, lower than the 4.3% increase in house purchase prices over the same period but one of the highest growth rates among European and OECD countries. In the euro area on average, rent prices rose by 1.3% over the same period.

Rental markets in the major cities of the Czech Republic have been impacted by the COVID-19 crisis, as measures introduced to contain the spread of the virus led to a near-complete freeze of tourism activities around the world (OECD, 2020[18]). As a result, many flats located in the centre of touristic cities such as Prague, which were used for short-term rentals through peer-to-peer accommodation rental Internet platforms, have been introduced into the long-term rental market, creating some downward pressure on rents. However, this could be short-lived, as uncertainties remain on medium- to long-term impacts of the COVID-19 crisis on rental markets and about whether these dwellings will return to the short-term market once tourism activity recovers.

Figure 1.6. Rent prices, change between Q1 2005 and Q4 2020

Rent price index, 2015=100, seasonally adjusted

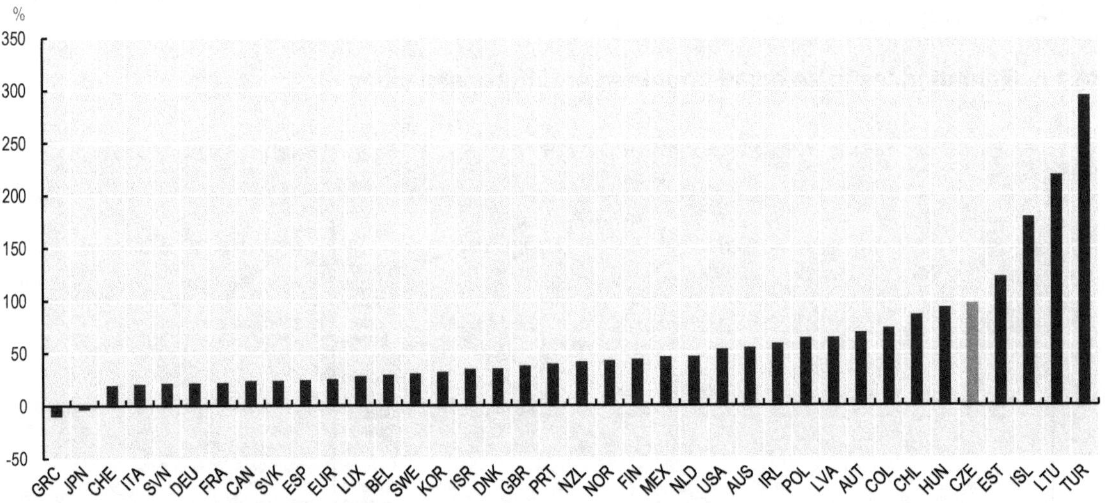

Note: Data for Q4 2020 were not available for Australia and New Zealand for which data for Q3 2020 were used.
Source: OECD (2021[12]), *Analytical House Price Indicators Database*, https://stats.oecd.org/.

Drivers pushing housing demand up in Czech cities are likely to withstand the COVID-19 crisis

While the COVID-19 pandemic is still unfolding, whether it will have a long-lasting impact on housing affordability will depend on many factors, including the duration of the pandemic and the extent of recovery packages. The impacts of the crisis also vary significantly across territories, for example depending on the region's exposure to tradeable sectors and global value chains, its specialisation such as tourism and its share of occupations amenable to remote working (OECD, 2020[19]). However, evidence from past pandemics suggests that the impacts on the housing market and the decline in house prices in cities are generally short-lived (Francke and Korevaar, 2021[20]). In particular, cities' resilience to major shocks and resulting urban change can drive house prices up back to their previous levels. The following section discusses the structural drivers of housing demand in cities in the Czech Republic.

Housing demand in the Czech Republic has been fuelled by various economic, financial and demographic factors

Some factors that have driven the strong demand for housing in cities are common to the Czech Republic.

Strong economic growth and rising real wages until 2020.

The Czech economy has been thriving in the past few years and economic growth has accelerated since 2013. In the years preceding the COVID-19 pandemic, national gross domestic product (GDP) expanded by 5.2% in 2017, 3.2% in 2018 and 2.3% in 2019. The Czech Republic's geographical location and openness to foreign direct investment – also driven by the country's accession to the European Union (EU) and single market – fostered integration to global value chains and higher productivity (OECD, 2020[21]). Combined with low unemployment and a tight labour market with a high level of job vacancies, this has contributed to an acceleration of wage growth, resulting in a convergence of incomes and GDP per capita towards the OECD average and rising living standards. In turn, the Czech Republic has maintained one of the lowest rates of inequality and poverty in the OECD (OECD, 2020[21]) (Figure 1.7).

Figure 1.7. Converging GDP per capita and low-income inequalities

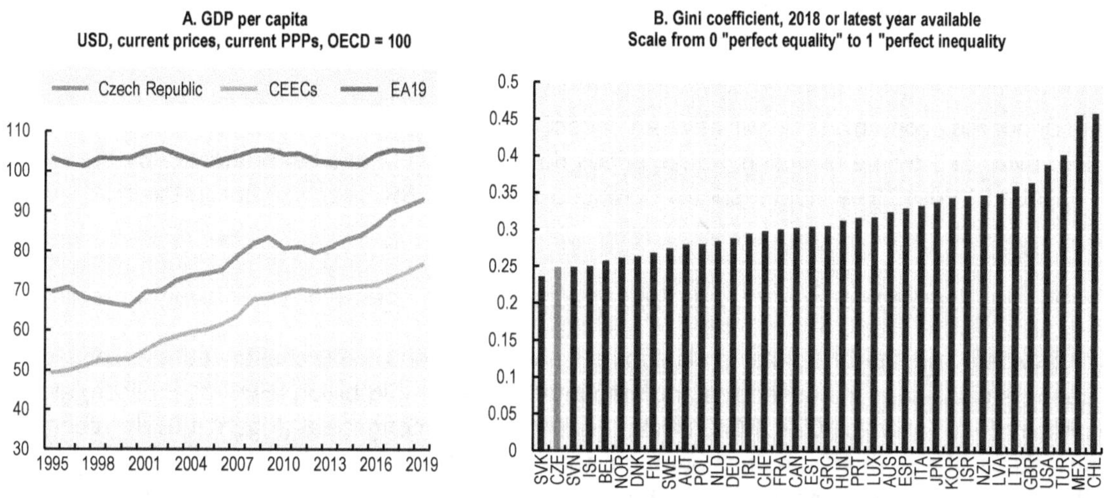

Note: Central and Eastern European countries (CEECs) are Hungary, Poland, the Slovak Republic and Slovenia.
Source: OECD (2020[22]), *Productivity Database*, https://stats.oecd.org/; OECD (OECD[23]), *Income Distribution Database*, https://stats.oecd.org/.

Figure 1.8. Economic sentiment and GDP forecasts for 2020 and 2021

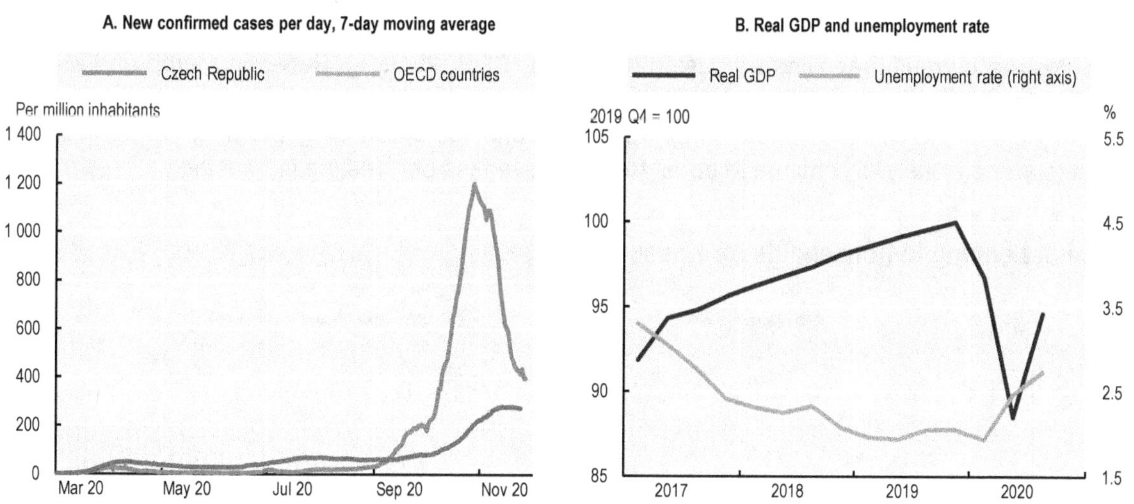

Source: OECD (2020[24]), *OECD Economic Outlook, Volume 2020 Issue 1*, https://dx.doi.org/10.1787/0d1d1e2e-en.

However, the COVID-19 pandemic and the resulting lockdown and containment measures that were put in place from March 2020 onwards have had a deep adverse economic impact, putting a halt to the continuous growth experienced in the past few years. In spring 2020, with restrictions to mobility and private consumption, retail sales and industrial output fell respectively by 9% and 11% year-on-year (OECD, 2020[24]). While the first wave of the outbreak was relatively well contained and recovery started when the initial lockdown ended in April 2020, the Czech Republic experienced a stronger second wave of the epidemic, which triggered renewed restrictions and a freeze in the recovery since September 2020. Unemployment also started to rise from its initially low levels, reaching 2.9% in the third quarter of 2020, although it remains very low in international comparison. GDP is estimated to have contracted by around 5.6% in 2020 and is expected to recover slowly, by 1.5% in 2021, and 3.3% in 2022 (OECD, 2020[21]). While a more prolonged lockdown could hamper recovery, a quicker-than-expected deployment of vaccines – which are for now expected to be widely deployed only in the second half of 2021 – and continued government support to companies could trigger higher confidence and stronger economic growth in the coming year.

Whether or not the economic crisis will have an impact on house prices in the long term is uncertain at this point. However, at the time of writing, house prices do not seem to have been affected by the crisis and have continued to rise. Real house prices increased by almost 6% year-on-year in the third quarter of 2020.

Favourable lending conditions, with low mortgage rates and high availability of credit.

According to data from the CNB, total lending to households for housing purchases represented more than three-quarters of all loans to households and amounted to CZK 1 436 billion (EUR 51.6 billion) at the end of December 2020 (of which CZK 1 343 billion, i.e. 94%, were mortgages) (Figure 1.9). In recent years, the high volume of new mortgages has been driven by low interest rates, household income growth and Czech households' continued preference for homeownership. While a record amount of housing loans had been granted to households in 2018 (CZK 232 billion of which CZK 187 billion [i.e. 80%)] in mortgages), credit growth has slowed down since then, due to a tightening of lending conditions introduced by the CNB in order to counter the "spiral between property prices and property purchase loans" (CNB, 2018[25]). The CNB introduced caps on the debt-to-income (DTI) ratio and the debt service-to-income (DSTI). From October 2018, debt should not exceed 9 times the net annual income of borrowers and the DSTI ratio should not exceed 45%. However, these prudential ratios are only recommendations and have no binding power, which limits their effectiveness (OECD, 2018[26]). The average size of loans provided for house purchases has also increased, mainly because of the increase in house prices. About one-fifth of Czech households are currently repaying a housing mortgage (CNB, 2019[27]). Between March and May 2020, the CNB cut policy rates 3 times, from 2.25% to 0.25%, and lowered the counter-cyclical buffer from 1.75% to 1% to help banks extend credit. Financial conditions for purchasing property, therefore, remain favourable and are likely to continue to boost the attractiveness of investing in housing.

Figure 1.9. Lending to households for house purchase

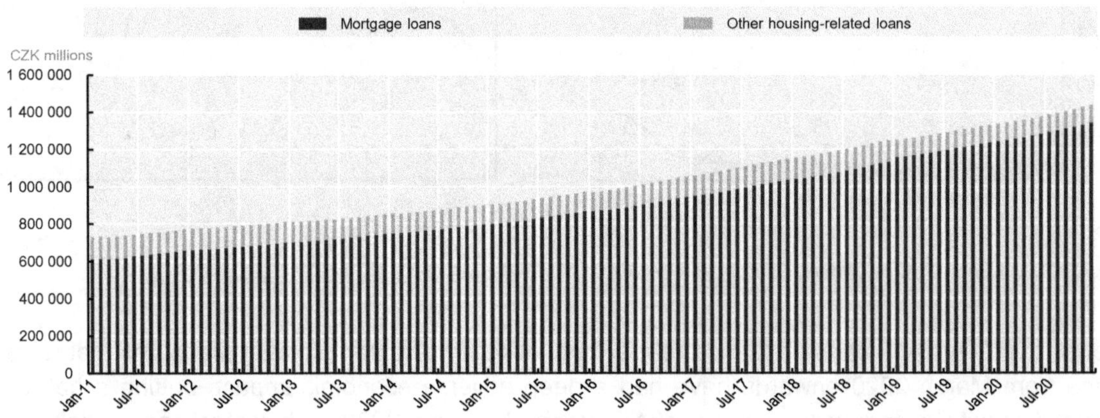

Source: CNB (2020[28]), *Czech National Bank Statistics*, https://www.cnb.cz/en/statistics/.

Changes in household composition and population ageing.

Demographic growth in the Czech Republic has been low and the size of households has been decreasing steadily. The average size of a Czech household reached 2.42 people in 2018 and the number of households increased to almost 4.4 million households in 2018, leading to more demand for housing. Furthermore, the Czech Republic is ageing more rapidly than most European countries, with the share of the population aged 65 years or more increasing by 5 percentage points between 2008 and 2018. Projections also show that the share of the population aged 80 years old or more is expected to increase from 4% of the total population today to more than 12% by 2060 (Figure 1.10). By 2040, about a quarter of the population is expected to be 65 years or older, compared with 18% of the population today (OECD, 2018[26]). While evidence of how population ageing affects house prices is ambiguous, population ageing does influence the type of housing demand, as the older and less mobile population has specific needs in terms of housing size and accessibility, for example. Adapting the existing housing stock to meet demand from an ageing population therefore implies home renovation and upgrading efforts.

Figure 1.10. Evolution of households in the Czech Republic

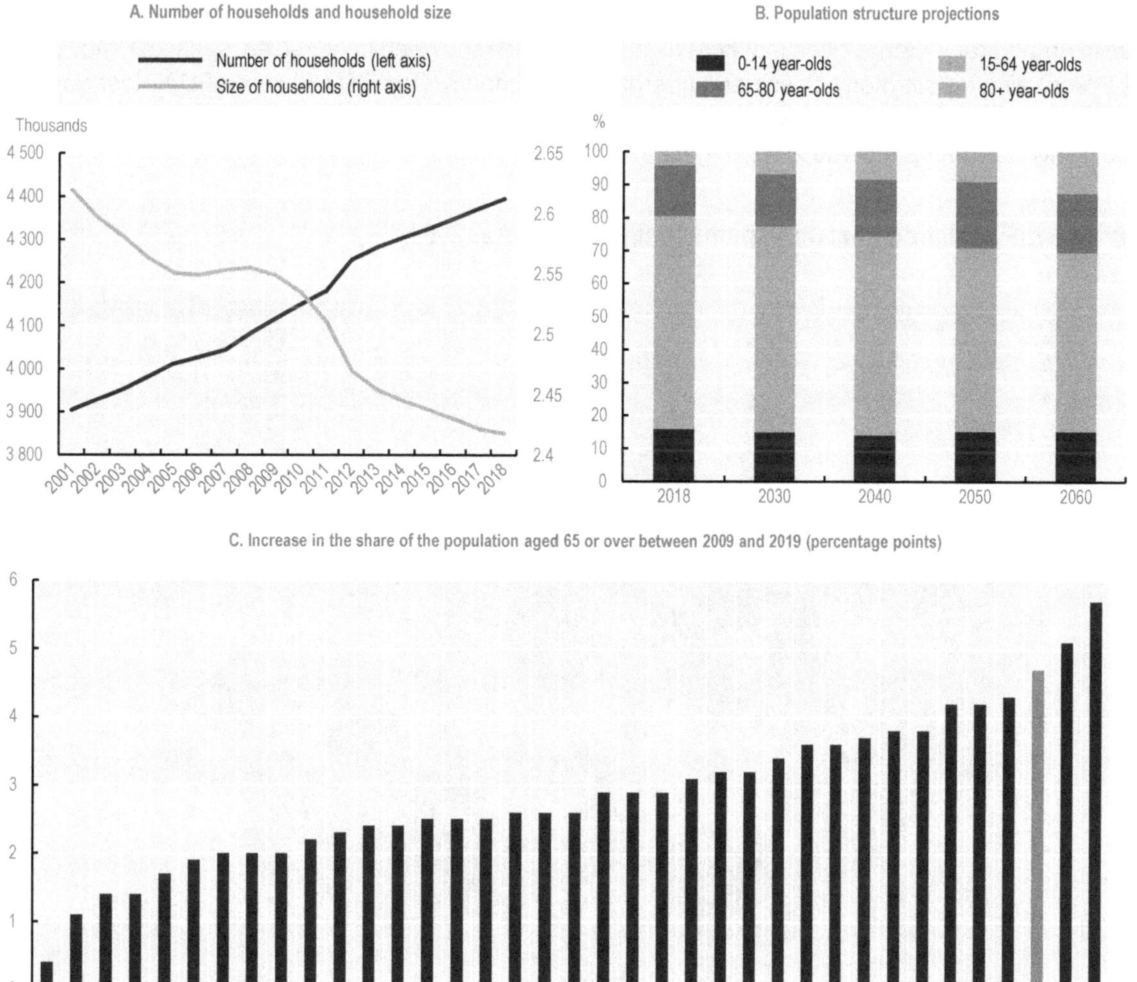

Source: ECB (2020[29]), *Statistical Data Warehouse*, https://sdw.ecb.europa.eu/home.do; OECD (2020[30]), *Population Statistics*, https://stats.oecd.org/.

However, some factors of housing demand are specific to cities

Whereas some factors influencing house prices are national, such as demographic trends, the availability of credit and the CNB's interest rate policy (discussed in the previous section), housing markets are by definition influenced by their location and involve a range of specific local factors. Cities are popular locations and attract people who want to benefit from the availability of jobs, education, lifestyles and cultural opportunities, as well as urban infrastructure, public goods and services.

The share of population living in cities and towns or semi-dense areas is lower than the average in high-income countries (22% in urban centres, 37% in towns and semi-dense areas and 41% in rural areas in the Czech Republic, compared with 49%, 27% and 24% respectively in high-income countries on average) (OECD/EC, 2020[31]). However, over the last decade in the Czech Republic, the population living in FUAs, i.e. a city and of its commuting zone (Dijkstra, Poelman and Veneri, 2019[32]), has increased faster than in the country overall. According to the Czech Statistical Office, the population in all Czech FUAs increased by 4.5% between 2009 and 2019, compared to only 1.8% in the Czech Republic in the same period (Czech Statistical Office, 2020[16]). The fastest increase in population over the last decade was registered in the FUAs of Brno, Ceske Budejovice, Pilsen and Prague. Prague expanded by 9.7% in 10 years and Brno, Pilsen and Ceske Budejovice rose by 5.7%, 5.4% and 5.3% respectively. Faster population growth in cities is due to inflows from rural areas to the main cities, as well as inflows of migrants from abroad who tend to settle in urban areas. Some cities that host high-quality and renowned universities, such as Brno, Olomouc and Pilsen, also attract many Czech and international students. Conversely, some FUAs lost population. This is the case of Ostrava and Most, for example, where the population decreased by 5.1% and 4.9% respectively between 2009 and 2019 (Figure 1.11).

Figure 1.11. Population change in municipalities of FUAs, 2009-19

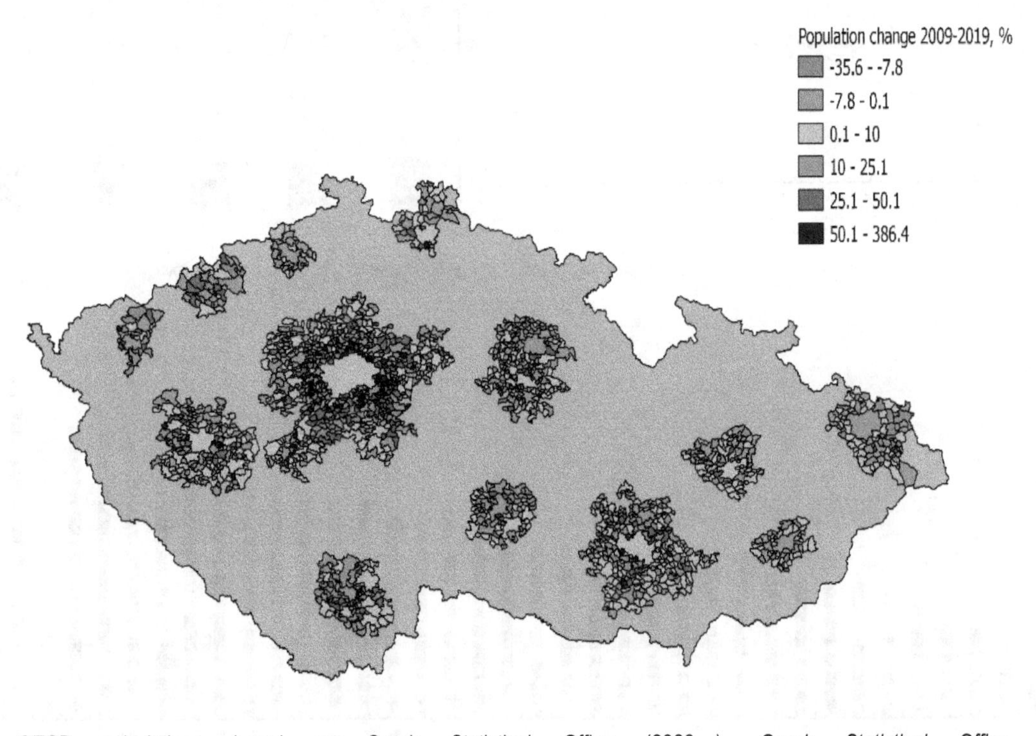

Source: OECD calculations based on Czech Statistical Office (2020[16]), *Czech Statistical Office Statistics*, https://www.czso.cz/csu/czso/statistics.

Some Czech cities are also very attractive to investors and demand for investment properties has been increasing – especially demand for prime properties by foreigners who have been able to purchase real estate in the Czech Republic without limitation since 2012 (IMF, 2018[33]). Prague, in particular, has become a mainstream destination for property investment in Europe (PwC/Urban Land Institute, 2017[34]). This has put more pressure on house prices in the past few years. Although the economic literature analysing the direct impact of foreign acquisition of real estate on domestic house prices remains scarce, there is cross-country evidence of a broad relationship between aggregate capital inflows and house prices, through the increased demand for housing, the increased money supply and liquidity due to capital inflows and the positive impact of capital inflows on economic activity, pushing house prices further up (Cavalleri, Cournède and Ziemann, 2019[35]).

The increase in tourism and the intensified use of short-term rental platforms has been fostered by the higher yield generated by short-term rentals compared with the yield generated on the long-term rental market. This has also led to a decline in available and affordable rental flats and a surge in rental prices in the capital city. In 2018, Prague was the 6th most visited city in Europe and 22nd in the world, with a total amount of 9.15 million tourists – ahead of other popular European destinations such as Amsterdam, Barcelona, Milan or Vienna (Euromonitor International, 2019[36]). In Prague, the share of peer-to-peer accommodation in the total hospitality accommodation capacity has been growing rapidly, from 34% in 2016 to almost 41% in 2018, almost matching the accommodation capacity of hotels (Deloitte, 2019[37]). While peer-to-peer listings account for less than 2% of Prague's total housing stock and are mostly concentrated in the historical centre, almost a quarter of Prague's Old Town flats are rented out for tourist short-term rentals (see Chapter 2 for examples of policies implemented by OECD countries to regulate holiday rentals).

The COVID-19 crisis put a sudden halt to touristic activities in the Czech Republic, as in all other OECD countries, significantly impacting the short-term rental market. Many short-term rental properties have remained vacant, while some owners have turned their properties into long-term rentals. While this could result in stabilisation or even a decrease in rent prices, the effects are likely to be modest and short-lived, given that these short-term rentals account for only a small share of total accommodations and that tourism activity is expected to pick up again when the COVID-19 crisis is under control.

An increasing share of the urban population lives outside urban centres, creating other social and environmental challenges

The Czech Republic has one of the highest shares of urban population residing outside urban centres. The decentralisation index, i.e. the percentage of population residing outside the high-density peaks of an urban area, is approximately 10% higher in the Czech Republic than in the average OECD country (OECD, 2018[38]). Between 2009 and 2019, in all Czech FUAs except for Most, the population increased faster in the commuting zones of the FUAs than in their core cities, indicating a phenomenon of urban sprawl (Figure 1.12).

Other indicators also confirm that Czech cities have been sprawling since 1990. Average population density, i.e. the average number of inhabitants in a km^2 of land of an urban area, has decreased by 11%, while decentralisation has increased by 13%. This has also been accompanied by an 8% increase in polycentricity, i.e. the number of high population density peaks in urban areas. These numbers mean that more urban centres have emerged but a greater number of urban residents have moved outside of them (Figure 1.13) (OECD, 2018[38]).

Figure 1.12. Population change in FUAs, core cities and commuting zones, 2009-19

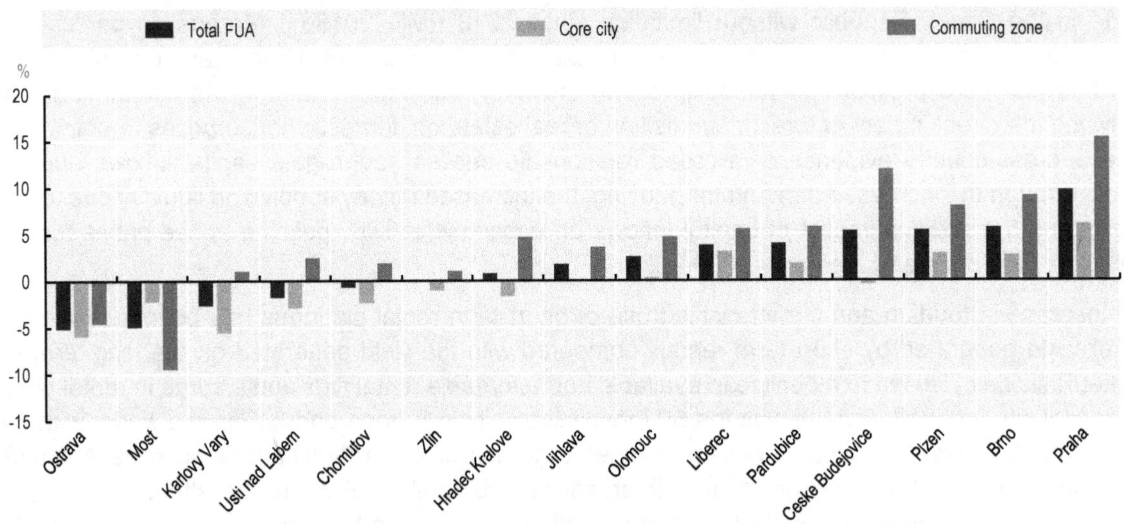

Source: Czech Statistical Office (2020[16]), *Czech Statistical Office Statistics*, https://www.czso.cz/csu/czso/statistics.

Figure 1.13. Change in urban sprawl indicators, 1990-2014

Relative change

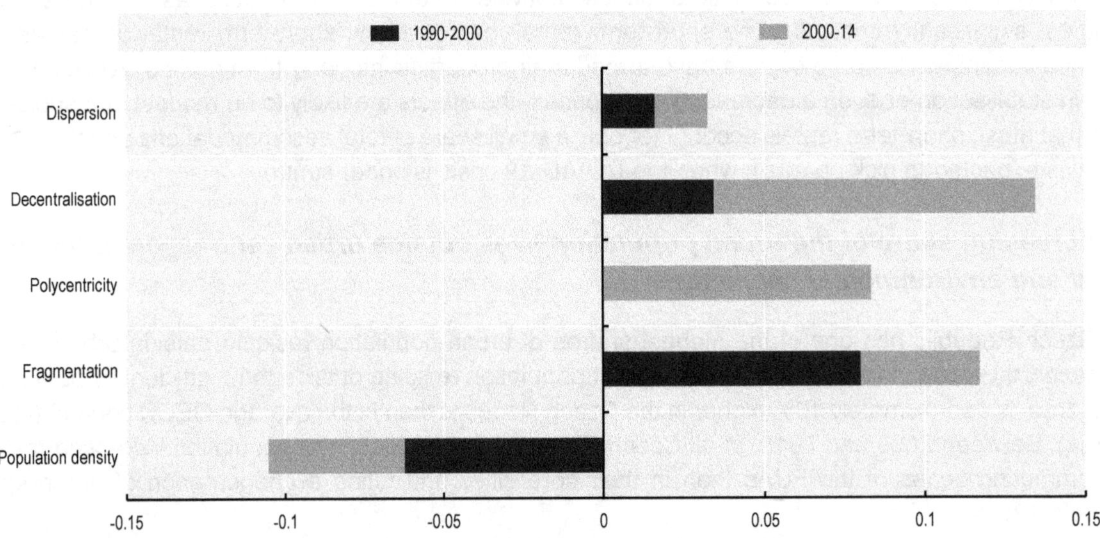

Note: Population density: average number of inhabitants per square kilometre (km²) of land. Dispersion: standard deviation of population density. Polycentricity: number of high population peaks in an urban area. Fragmentation: number of urban fabric fragments per km² of built-up area. Decentralisation: percentage of population residing outside areas of peak density.
Source: OECD (2018[38]), *Rethinking Urban Sprawl: Moving Towards Sustainable Cities*, https://doi.org/10.1787/9789264189881-en.

Urban sprawl has significant environmental, economic and social consequences, including higher emissions from road transport (as sprawled cities are characterised by larger distances between homes and jobs, more likely to be covered by car), and higher costs of providing key public services (such as water supply, electricity and public transport, which are more expensive to provide in fragmented areas). Main cities do have integrated transport systems and public transport is the main mode used by residents in Prague and Ostrava (70% and 53.4% of residents respectively). However, the increase in suburbanisation, coupled with the rise in households' incomes, has resulted in an increase in car ownership in the Czech Republic. In Prague, car ownership grew by more than 40% between 2010 and 2019, leading to congestion, noise and air pollution (OECD, 2018[39]; Czech Statistical Office, n.d.[40]). In the outer zone of the city of Prague, car traffic volume increased over the past 10 years, while it decreased in the centre of the city (Figure 1.14).

Figure 1.14. Car traffic volume has gone up in Prague's outer zone, 2006-16

Passenger transport in Prague

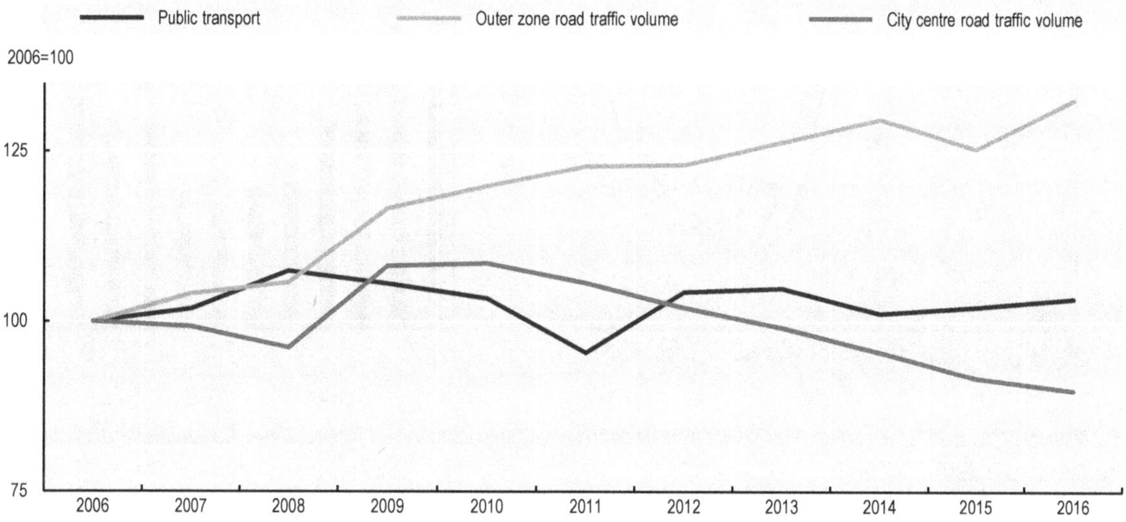

Note: Public transport: index based on the number of passengers transported. Traffic volume: index based on the number of vehicles over the 24 hours of an average workday. City centre: bounded by Petřín in the west, Letná in the north, Riegrovy sady in the east and Vyšehrad in the south (the Strahov and Mrázovka tunnels lie outside the central cordon). Outer zone: traffic volume is measured where the main roads and motorways enter the city centre.
Source: City of Prague (n.d.[41]), *Prague Transportation Yearbook*, Various years.

Czech cities face a shortage of housing supply

Started and completed dwellings have not caught up with their previously high levels

When housing supply is elastic enough, it ensures that the economy responds to housing needs in a timely manner without large price increases, thus underpinning housing affordability. However, the high and growing demand for housing in Czech cities has not been met by a sufficient increase in housing supply. Construction activity declined after the global financial crisis and has yet to recover. The numbers of started and completed dwellings per 1 000 inhabitants decreased sharply between 2008 and 2013. Although these numbers picked up again since 2014, they have not caught up yet with the levels reached before 2008. In 2019, dwelling completions rose by 7.6% from the previous year to 36 406 units, following annual increases of 18.5% in 2018, 4.6% in 2017 and 8.9% in 2016, according to the Czech Statistical Office (Czech Statistical Office, 2020[16]). Likewise, dwelling starts were up by 16.8%, reaching 38 677 units in 2019. However, the number of flats starts and completions per 1 000 inhabitants currently remains below their 2008 levels, with construction responding only very slowly to the increased demand for housing in recent years (Figure 1.15).

Furthermore, according to calculations from the MMR, the total stock of housing decreased between 2011 and 2017. Not enough new dwellings were built to compensate for some of the wear and tear of old dwellings or the change in use from residential to commercial, for example. While the stock of housing increased in 2018 and 2019, it has not gone back to its previous level. The COVID-19 pandemic also froze all construction projects in spring 2020, leading to a sharp decrease in completed dwellings for 2020 (Figure 1.15).

Figure 1.15. Number of dwellings started and completed in the Czech Republic

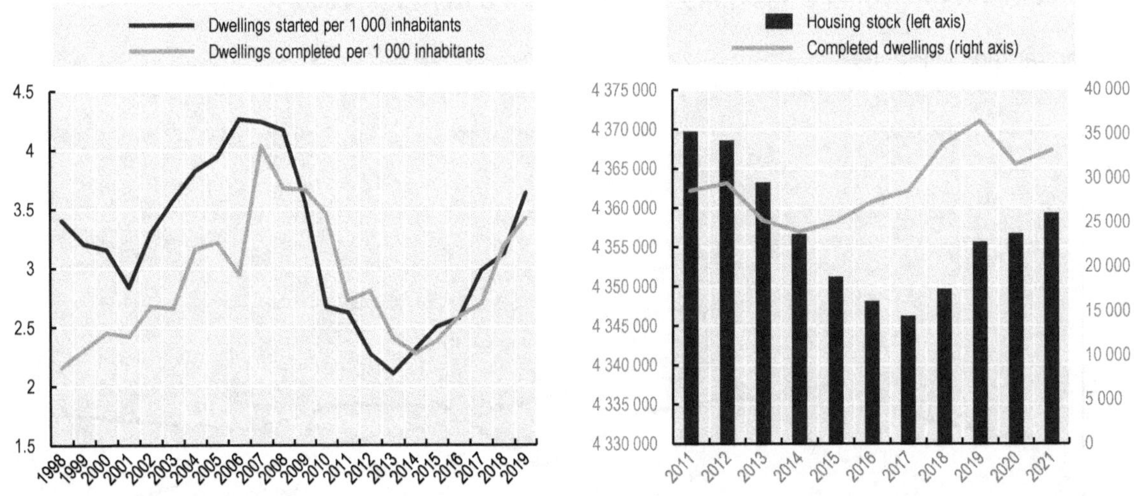

Source: Ministry of Regional Development and OECD calculations based on Czech Statistical Office (2020[16]), *Czech Statistical Office Statistics*, https://www.czso.cz/csu/czso/statistics.

Construction activity does not happen where it is most needed

Such construction numbers at the national level hide wide variations among territories and cities. While about 20% of all completed dwellings were built in Prague (around 6 700 completed flats and family houses in 2019), the number of dwellings completed per 1 000 inhabitants is still low, with just above 5 completed dwellings per 1 000 inhabitants. In most major Czech cities, the number of completed dwellings per 1 000 inhabitants in 2019 was also below 5. The only exceptions among the core cities of the 15 Czech FUAs are Pilsen, Olomouc and Ceske Budejovice, where there were 7.4, 7.9 and 8.4 completed dwellings per 1 000 inhabitants respectively in 2019. Furthermore, in all Czech FUAs except Olomouc, the number of completed dwellings per 1 000 inhabitants was higher in the commuting zones of FUAs than in core cities, mirroring the higher population increase in the commuting zones and confirming the suburbanisation trend discussed earlier (Figure 1.16).

Furthermore, the OECD-MMR housing survey shows that housing development in the Czech Republic has been unrelated to price levels. When housing construction does happen, it does not seem to focus on high-priced areas. Figure 1.17 shows the relationship between a municipality's house prices and the number of building permits per 1 000 inhabitants that were issued between 2015 and 2019. There is no indication that municipalities with higher price levels have experienced increased construction activity, which suggests that the growth in demand (reflected in higher prices) has not been buffered by an increase in supply. In contrast, many municipalities with low price levels experienced considerable housing development. In these municipalities, there is therefore a risk that this excess housing development creates undesired side-effects in terms of urban sprawl as described earlier. This pattern of non-correlation between house prices and construction levels is also observed at the level of the FUA. The two FUAs where the most building permits were issued (Liberec and Mladá Boleslav) have only average housing prices, while Prague did not have a significant amount of issued building permits even though it registers the highest housing prices (Figure 1.18).

Figure 1.16. Completed dwellings per 1 000 inhabitants in FUAs in the Czech Republic

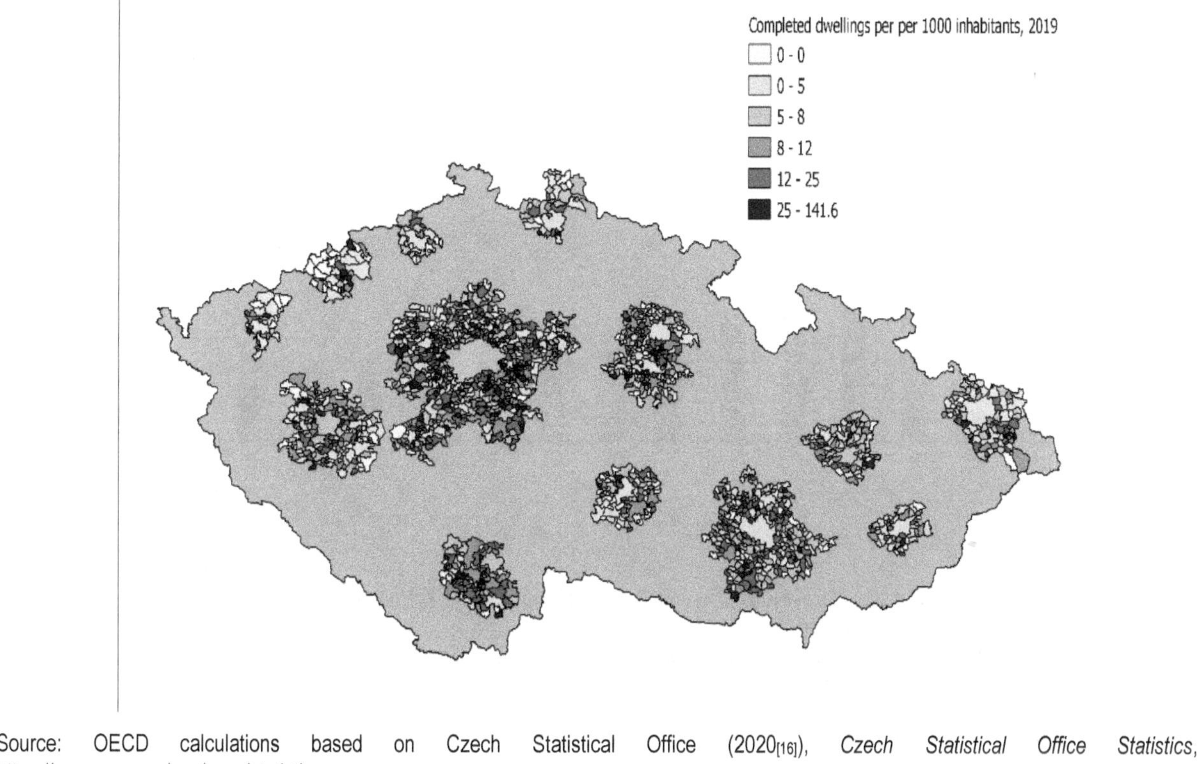

Source: OECD calculations based on Czech Statistical Office (2020[16]), *Czech Statistical Office Statistics*, https://www.czso.cz/csu/czso/statistics.

Figure 1.17. No correlation between price levels and construction activity (respondent municipalities), 2015-19

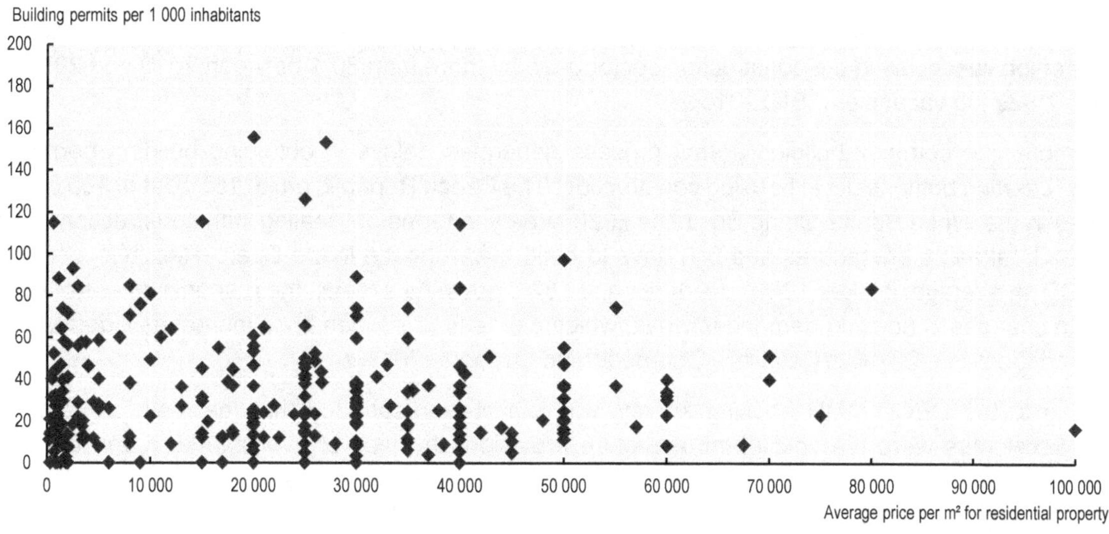

Note: The vertical axis shows the number of building permits granted during 2015-19 per 1 000 inhabitants. The horizontal axis provides average residential property prices as estimated by local officials.
Source: OECD/MMR (2020[42]), *OECD-MMR Housing Survey of Municipalities in the Czech Republic*.

Figure 1.18. No correlation between house price levels and construction activity in FUAs in the Czech Republic

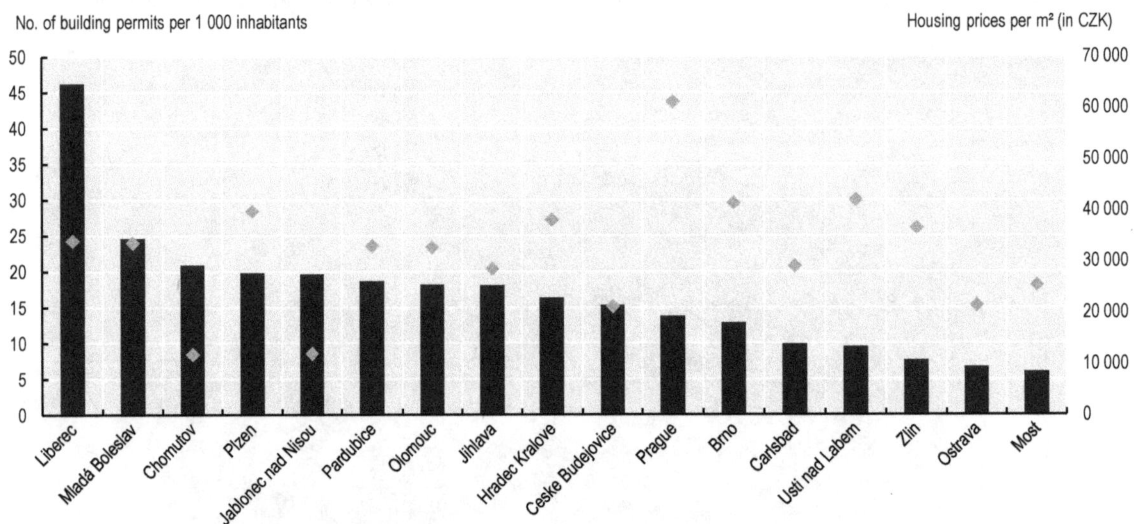

Note: The left-side axis shows the number of building permits granted during 2015-19 per 1 000 inhabitants. The right-side axis provides average residential property prices as estimated by local officials.
Source: OECD/MMR (2020[42]), *OECD-MMR Housing Survey of Municipalities in the Czech Republic.*

Private sector housing supply faces several constraints

Several factors can explain the shortage of housing supply in the Czech Republic. First, partly due to a very low unemployment rate (2.1% of the labour force in the fourth quarter of 2019 – the lowest unemployment rate among all OECD countries), there has been a shortage of qualified workers in the construction sector. This made it difficult for developers and local governments to find contractors and led to lengthy construction times and higher construction costs. The overall number of construction companies has actually decreased (with a decline in company births and an increase in company deaths), while the number of job vacancies in the construction sector grew by more than 80% between 2010 and 2015 (from 4 239 to 7 689 job vacancies) (EC, 2018[43]).

Furthermore, the complex building permit process generates delays in obtaining building permits and licences, creating bottlenecks in housing construction. The Czech Republic ranks 157th out of 190 countries surveyed in the World Bank's Doing Business 2020 survey in terms of "dealing with construction permits" (2019[44]). It takes 21 procedures and 246 days to build a warehouse in the Czech Republic, whereas in the OECD on average, it takes 12.7 procedures and 152.3 days. As a result, the responsiveness of housing supply to changes in housing demand is weak, which can lead to sudden price increases if demand rises (Bétin and Ziemann, 2019[45]; Cavalleri, Cournède and Özsöğüt, 2019[46]).

According to the OECD-MMR housing survey, municipalities responded that the main constraints for private developers were the cost of infrastructure provision, the lack of available land and the lack of infrastructure capacity (Figure 1.19). In line with the aforementioned World Bank data, the complicated and lengthy building permit process also ranked high on the list of constraints.

Figure 1.19. Main constraints for private developers

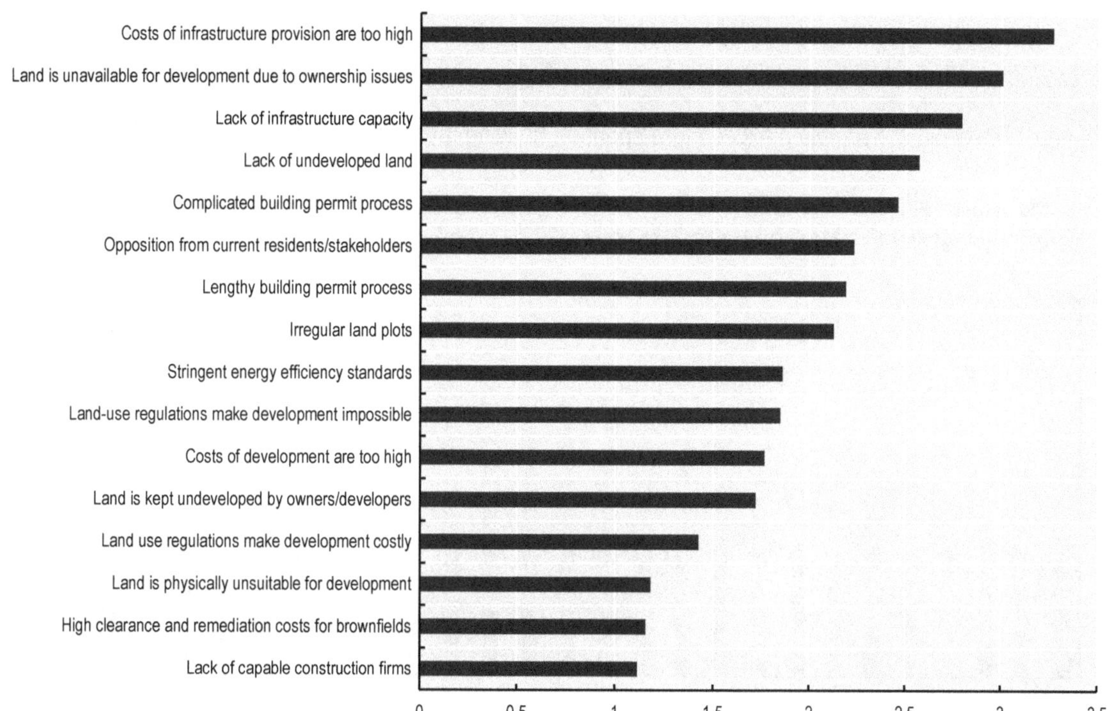

Note: The horizontal axis shows the average score of each constraint based on a Likert scale ranging from 0 for "no importance" to 5 for "very high importance".
Source: OECD/MMR (2020[42]), *OECD-MMR Housing Survey of Municipalities in the Czech Republic*.

Living in cities imposes a heavy financial burden on Czech households

As discussed previously, housing affordability is not only about the ability to buy or rent a house but also the ability to live in it and to have enough remaining income to meet other basic needs. Two common indicators in this regard are: i) the share of housing-related expenditures (i.e. rent or mortgage, water, electricity, gas and other housing-related expenditures) relative to overall final consumption expenditures of a household; and ii) the housing cost overburden, which is the share of households that spend more than 40% of their disposable household income on rent or mortgage.

Housing-related expenditures put a substantial burden on Czech households

Housing costs take up a large share of the budget of Czech households and represent their largest single expenditure. In 2018, Czech households on average devoted 26.5% of their expenditures to housing, i.e. to rents or imputed rents, insurance, mandatory services and charges, maintenance and repairs, taxes and the costs of utilities (water, electricity, gas and heating). This share is higher than the OECD average, where housing-related expenditure constituted 22.3% of final household expenditure, and it is one of the highest shares among all OECD countries (Figure 1.20). This share also represented an increase from 22.8% of final household consumption expenditure in 2000.

A relatively small share of Czech households' expenditure goes towards rents due to the large share of outright owners. Only 2.9% of final household consumption is spent on actual rents, compared to about 4% in the OECD on average. Spending on imputed rents, i.e. the estimated rent that owner-occupiers theoretically pay to themselves, accounts for 13.9% of final consumption in the Czech Republic, slightly above the OECD average of 13%. However, Czech households dedicate a relatively large share of spending to electricity, gas and other fuels (6.8% of final consumption, much higher than the OECD average of 4.0%).

Figure 1.20. Total housing expenditure as share of final consumption expenditure of households

Share of final household consumption expenditure spent on housing, by item, OECD countries, 2018

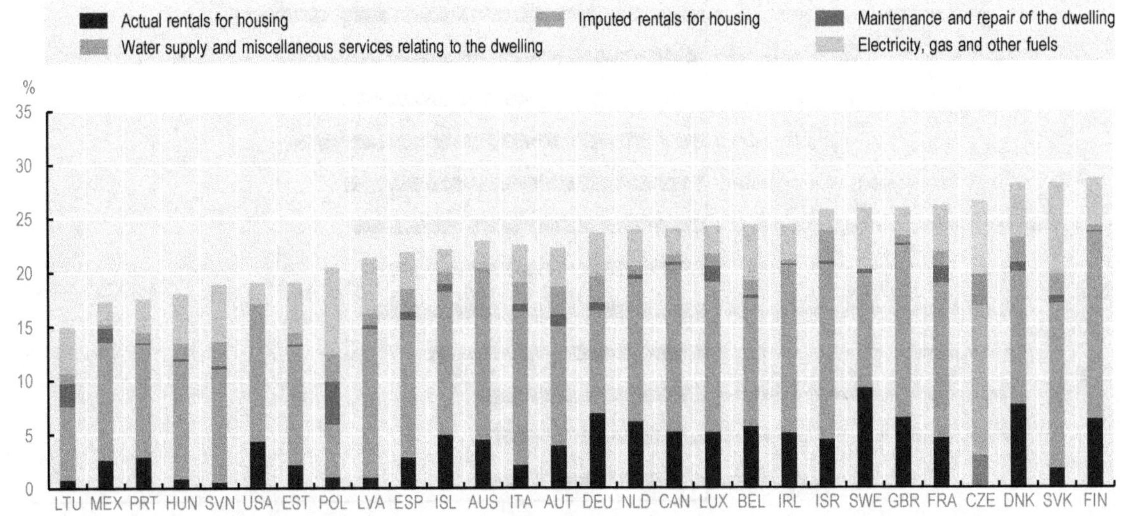

Note: Data cover final consumption expenditure.
Source: OECD (n.d.[47]) *National Accounts database*, https://stats.oecd.org/.

Total housing expenditure also accounts for a high share of Czech households' disposable income, suggesting that housing costs create strong financial pressure on Czech households. In 2018, the housing consumption of Czech households accounted for 20.2% of their net adjusted disposable income – one of the highest shares among all OECD countries (Figure 1.21).

Figure 1.21. Household housing consumption as a share of households' net adjusted disposable income, 2018

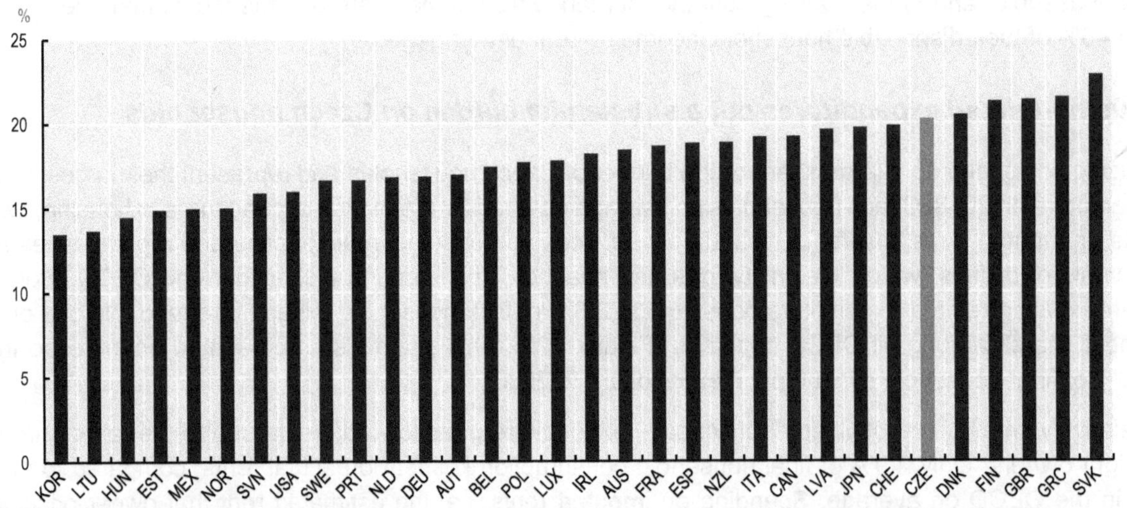

Note: Data are for 2018, except for Greece, Japan, Korea, Mexico, New Zealand, Switzerland and the United States for which data are for 2017.
Source: OECD (n.d.[47]) *National Accounts database*, https://stats.oecd.org/.

According to the EU Statistics on Income and Living Conditions (EU-SILC) (2020[48]), the financial burden created by housing costs for Czech households is particularly heavy for vulnerable groups and more so than in the EU on average (Figure 1.22), particularly for:

- Households at risk of poverty (i.e. those with an income below 60% of the median national income) that spend almost half of their disposable income (43.9%) to cover housing costs.
- Single people, who spend 33.9% of their disposable income on housing costs.
- People aged 65 and above, who spend more than a third of their disposable income on housing costs (34.5%): a category of elderly "asset-rich but cash-poor" people has emerged, i.e. people over 65 years old who in their large majority are outright homeowners as a result of the transition from communism or own their homes without paying any mortgages but who often lack the income or savings to pay for housing-related costs, such as maintenance or energy.
- Single parents, who spend more than a third of their disposable income on rents, mortgages and other housing-related costs (35.4%).

Figure 1.22. Share of total housing costs in disposable household income, by type of household and income group, Czech Republic and EU28

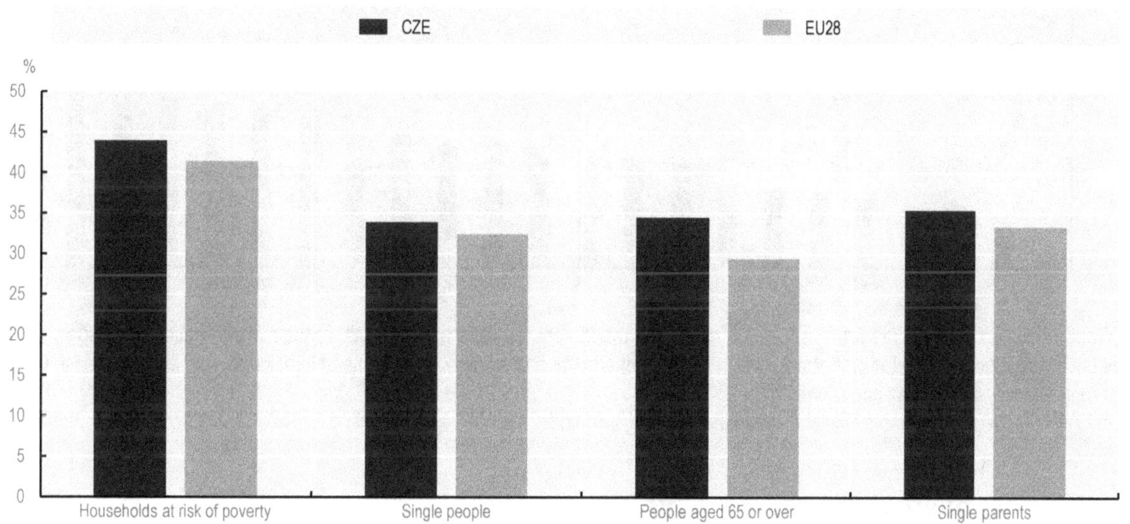

Source: Eurostat (2020[48]), *Eurostat Income and Living Conditions*, https://ec.europa.eu/eurostat/web/income-and-living-conditions/data/database.

In line with the fact that Czech households spend relatively little on rent only (actual and imputed), Czech households are also among the least likely in the OECD to be "overburdened" by housing costs, i.e. to spend more than 40% of their disposable household income on housing, when taking into account rents and mortgage costs only. In 2018, about 2.8% of Czech tenants and 1.6% of homeowners with a mortgage spent more than 40% of their disposable income on rent or mortgage. Even low-income tenants and homeowners with a mortgage are very unlikely to be overburdened by housing costs (7.1% and 10.4% of households respectively – much less than low-income households in the OECD on average) (OECD, 2020[6]).

However, housing costs other than rent and mortgage costs (e.g. insurance costs, mandatory services and charges, regular maintenance and repair, taxes and utilities) increase considerably the financial burden on households, especially on low-income households. Whereas the poorest Czech households were among the least likely across the OECD to face housing cost overburden when considering only mortgage payments and rents, they are among the most likely to face a housing cost overburden when all housing-related costs are taken into account. In 2018, almost three-quarters (73.7%) of households in the bottom quintile that were owners with a mortgage spent more than 40% of their disposable income on total housing costs, while the share is two-thirds (66.8%) for low-income renters on the private market (OECD, 2020[6]) (Figure 1.23).

Figure 1.23. Total housing cost overburden rate among low-income tenants in the Czech Republic and selected OECD countries

Share of tenants in the bottom quintile of the income distribution paying more than 40% of disposable income on rent, and share of tenants in the bottom quintile of the income distribution paying more than 40% on total housing costs, percent, 2018 or latest year available

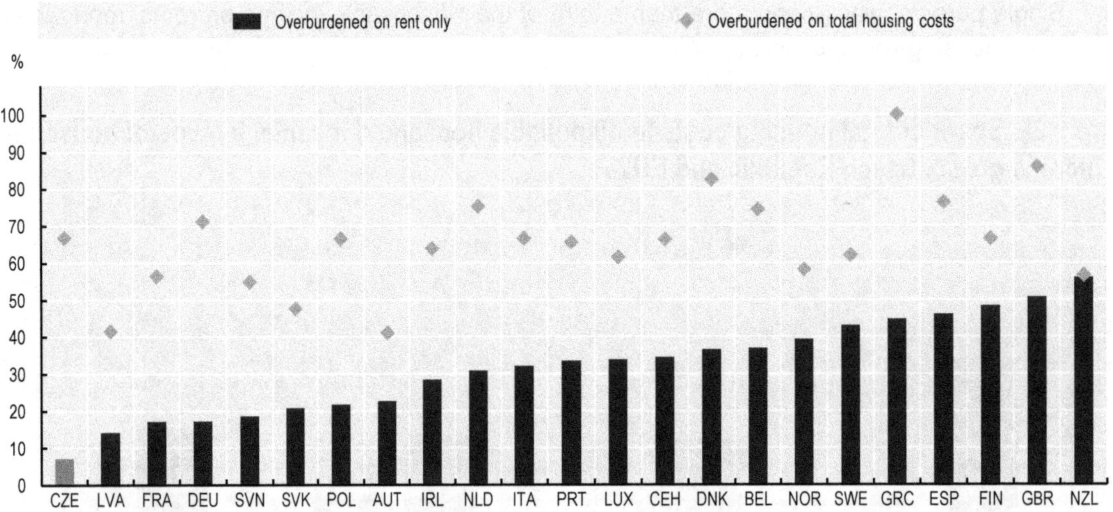

Note: Total housing costs include rents, structural insurance, mandatory services and charges, regular maintenance and repair, taxes and utilities (including electricity, water, gas and heating). In the Netherlands and Norway, no tenants at subsidised rate are included in the private market rent category due to data limitations.
Source: OECD (2020[6]), *Affordable Housing Database*, http://oe.cd/ahd.

Housing cost overburden rates are higher in cities

The housing cost overburden rate varies at the local level and is higher in cities in the Czech Republic. Analysis reveals that the overburden rate in the Czech Republic increases with the degree of urbanisation. In 2018, the housing cost overburden was the lowest in rural areas (4.4%), higher in towns and suburbs (7.0%) and the highest in cities (12.9%). The share of households overburdened by housing costs in cities is therefore 8.5 percentage points higher than in rural areas. This premium for living in cities in the Czech Republic is one of the highest among European countries, where on average the share of overburdened households is 3.7 percentage points higher in cities than in rural areas (Figure 1.24).

Furthermore, households in cities, towns and suburbs are more likely to be unable to keep their house adequately warm than in rural areas: 3.5% of households in cities, towns and suburbs, compared with 2.4% in rural areas. Several factors could be at play in urban areas: the higher costs of living, which makes it more difficult for households to pay all their bills; the relatively high share of poor population in cities; and the fact that the older building stock in cities is less energy efficient (see the section on housing quality below). In towns and suburbs, this could also be due to lower building density, resulting in higher heat dissipation (EU Energy Poverty Observatory, 2020[49]).

Figure 1.24. Housing cost overburden by degree of urbanisation, European countries, 2018

Share of people living in households where total housing costs represent more than 40% of disposable income

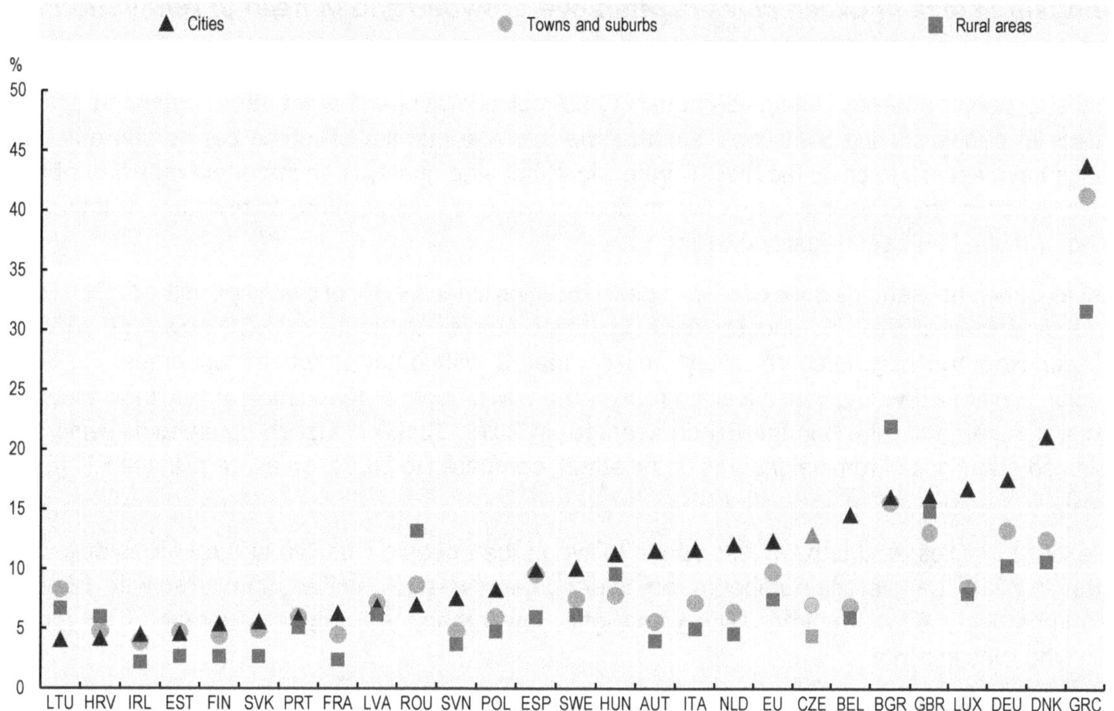

Source: Eurostat (2020[48]), *Eurostat Income and Living Conditions*, https://ec.europa.eu/eurostat/web/income-and-living-conditions/data/database.

Figure 1.25. Urban residents are more likely to face energy poverty

Inability to keep home warm and arrears on utility bills in the Czech Republic, by urban density

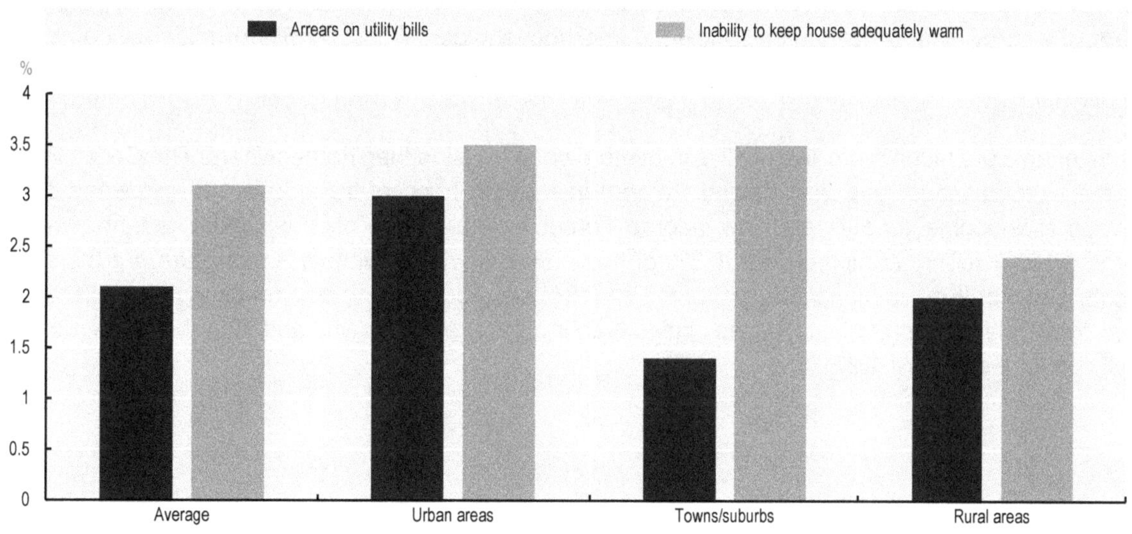

Source: EU Energy Poverty Observatory (2020[49]), *Member State Report: Czech Republic*, https://www.energypoverty.eu/sites/default/files/downloads/observatory-documents/20-06/extended_member_state_report_-_czechia.pdf.

The housing stock in Czech cities is often old and in need of energy efficiency improvements

The housing stock in Czech cities is often overcrowded and in need of renovation

Housing should offer not only a place to sleep and rest but also safety, privacy and personal space that responds to people's needs. Alongside housing cost considerations, it is therefore critical to assess the adequacy of people's living conditions, such as the average number of rooms per person and whether dwellings have access to basic facilities. Furthermore, housing quality is an important indicator of housing affordability, as many households that live in poor conditions cannot afford to maintain or improve their dwelling or move to a better-quality dwelling.

Almost all Czech households have access to basic facilities since 99.3% of dwellings in the Czech Republic offer private access to an indoor flushing toilet, more than the OECD average of 95.6%. The Czech Republic also fares relatively well compared with other European countries: 7.7% of the population lived in a dwelling with a leaking roof, damp walls, floors or foundation or rats in window frames or floors, compared to 13.6% in the EU on average. In 2018, 22.6% of Czech households living in cities complained about noise from neighbours or the street, compared to 28.5% on average in the EU (Eurostat, 2020[48]).

People living in cities tend to have less space to live in than people who live in rural areas or towns and suburbs. In 2018, the average number of rooms per person was 1.4 in cities, compared with 1.5 in towns and suburbs, and 1.6 in rural areas. This was slightly lower than the European average of 1.6 rooms per person who lives in a city.

Overcrowding also measures the number of rooms per household member but also taking into account the household composition such as the age, gender and relationship of household members. It is an important indicator, as evidence shows that living in an overcrowded dwelling can affect the physical and mental health of household members, as well as children's social and emotional development. Moreover, living in an overcrowded space corresponds with a higher likelihood of child maltreatment and accidents in the home. A dwelling is defined as overcrowded if it has an insufficient number of rooms relative to the households' composition (OECD, 2021[50]). A relatively high share of Czech households lives in overcrowded dwellings: 11.6% of the Czech households in 2019, slightly above the OECD average rate of 11.0%. Overcrowding is not limited to low-income households. Almost 12.5% of middle-income Czech households live in overcrowded dwellings, compared with an OECD average of around 10% (Figure 1.26) (OECD, 2020[6]).

Czech tenants are much more likely to live in overcrowded housing than homeowners. The Czech Republic has the second widest gap (just behind Poland) in the likelihood of living in an overcrowded dwelling between low-income tenants and low-income homeowners: 39.4% of low-income tenants live in an overcrowded dwelling, compared with 8.3% of homeowners with or without a mortgage. As the share of tenants is higher in cities than in the rest of the country, and housing size also tends to be smaller in cities, overcrowding is more prevalent in Czech cities than in rural areas or towns and suburbs, as in most other OECD countries (Figure 1.27).

Figure 1.26. Overcrowding rates in households across the income distribution, 2019 or latest year available

Share of overcrowded households, by quintiles of the income distribution

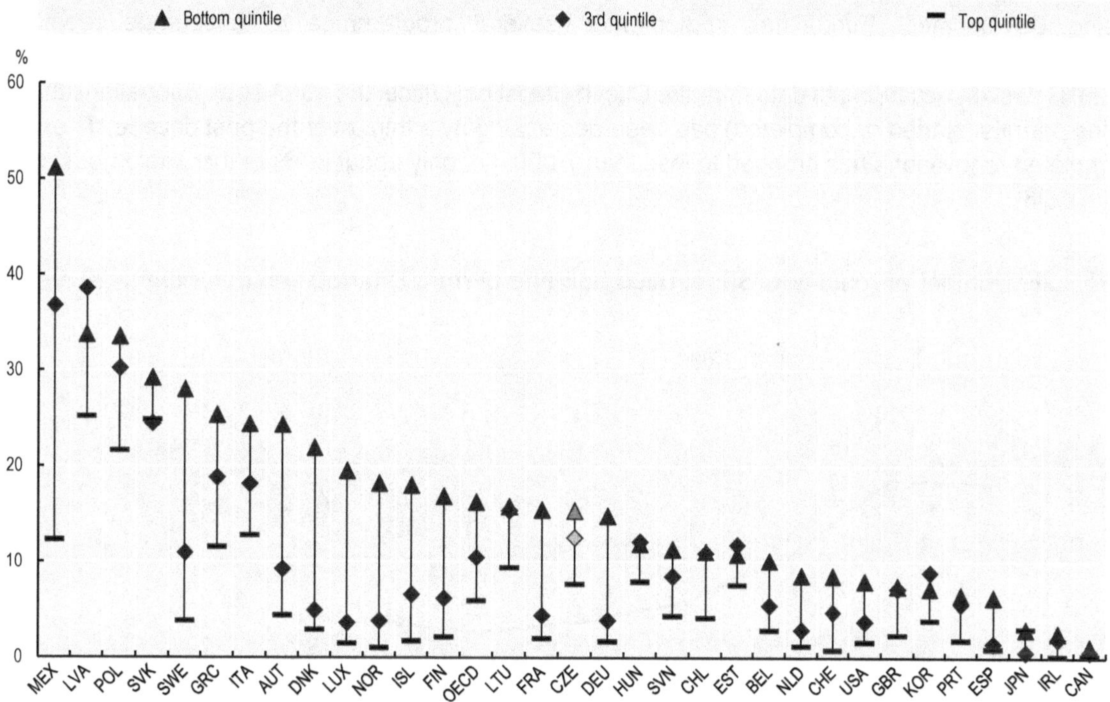

Source: OECD (2020[6]), *Affordable Housing Database*, http://oe.cd/ahd.

Figure 1.27. Overcrowding rate by degree of urbanisation, European countries

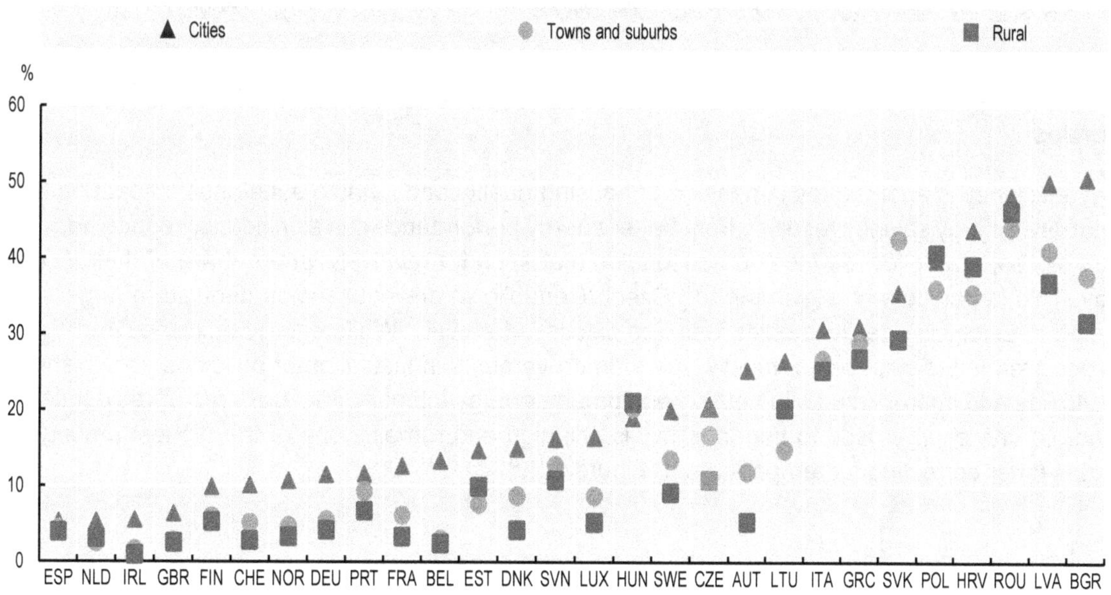

Source: Eurostat (2020[48]), *Eurostat Income and Living Conditions*, https://ec.europa.eu/eurostat/web/income-and-living-conditions/data/database.

Furthermore, a key issue with housing quality in cities in the Czech Republic is the physical deterioration of real estates, including buildings and neglected public spaces. According to the 2011 Population and Housing Census, the average age of occupied residential buildings in the Czech Republic was 52.4 years for multi-unit buildings and 49.3 years for family houses, which is older than the average age of buildings in the EU (Office of the Government, 2019[51]). The State Investment Support Fund (formerly called State Housing Development Fund) has implemented several programmes to encourage repairs and modernisation of housing (e.g. the Panel 2013+ programme, see Chapter 2 for other examples and more details). However, according to data from the Czech Statistical Office, the number of renovations that need building permits (started or completed) has been decreasing by a third over the past decade. The number of completed renovations has dropped to less than 7 000, i.e. only about 0.1% of the whole housing stock (Figure 1.28).

Figure 1.28. Number of renovations that need building permits, started and completed, 2010-19

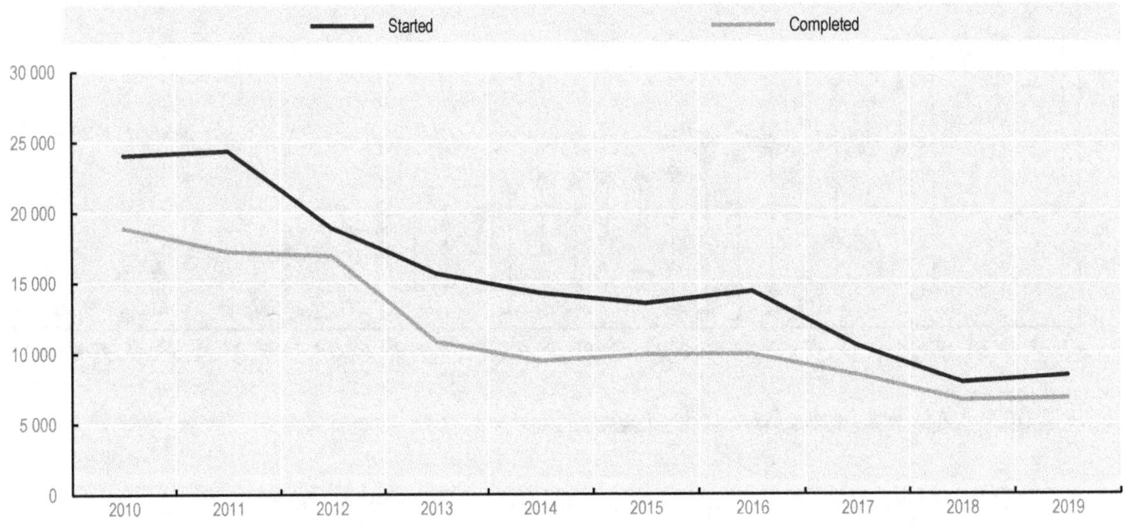

Source: Czech Statistical Office (2020[16]), *Czech Statistical Office Statistics*, https://www.czso.cz/csu/czso/statistics.

Housing in the Czech Republic is one of the least energy efficient among OECD countries

Energy efficiency is another key dimension of housing quality and it has a substantial impact on housing affordability. Energy savings resulting from better energy performance can significantly reduce households' energy bill, especially for low-income households that spend a relatively larger share of their income on energy. This is particularly relevant in the Czech Republic where households dedicate a large share of spending to electricity, gas and other fuels (as discussed earlier). While energy efficiency improvements have occurred in the past years, mostly due to improvements in insulation of buildings, refurbishment of old buildings and improvements in heating equipment, energy intensity per floor area of residential space heating, i.e. the energy used to heat one m², is still high and remains one of the highest among OECD countries (after correcting for temperatures) (Figure 1.29).

Figure 1.29. Energy intensity per floor area of residential space heating, temperature corrected, 2000-19, in selected OECD countries

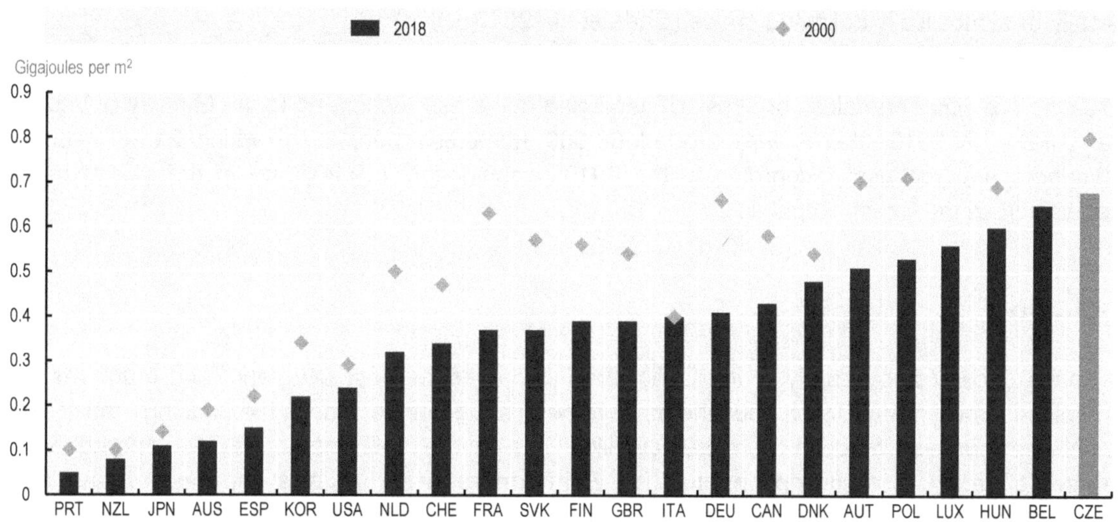

Note: Data is not available for 2000 for Belgium and Luxembourg.
Source: IEA (n.d.[52]), *IEA Data and Statistics*, https://www.iea.org/data-and-statistics/charts/energy-intensity-per-floor-area-of-residential-space-heating-in-selected-iea-countries-2000-2018.

Barriers to the housing market leave some social groups in substandard housing

As discussed previously, private rental accommodations rented at market prices have become financially inaccessible to many Czech households. Tenants are usually required to pay several months of rent in advance in the form of a safety deposit, which many cannot afford. Accessing municipal social housing also often turns out to be difficult, due to limited provision of social housing and long waiting lists (see more details on social housing provision in Chapter 2).

As a result, many households have no choice but to turn to alternative housing with substandard conditions, such as dormitories. Living conditions in these dormitories are generally very poor. Dormitories are flats or rooms, most often in private buildings, where residents do not have standard rental contracts, do not receive a local residence permit, and frequently pay overpriced rents for small and low-quality spaces (e.g. shared kitchen, shared sanitation facilities, overcrowding, badly insulated with energy leaks) poorly maintained by their private owners. Tenants in these types of housing do not benefit from legal protection and are often offered short-term tenancy agreements, although in most cases these dormitories are used as long-term housing solutions. Rent levels in dormitories are generally high relative to the housing quality that they offer and can even exceed the rent levels of standard rental flats. As residents in dormitories have few alternative options to find housing, they are also exposed to predatory practices by landlords who can impose high fines for minor violations of the rental contract or neglect essential repairs. Furthermore, people who have been living in this type of alternative housing often face stigma and discrimination when they later attempt to access the private rental market, which locks them in precarious housing in the long term.

Within the 758 municipalities that provided information on dormitories as part of the OECD-MMR housing survey, there are 555 privately-run dormitories, which are home to approximately 0.7% of the population in these municipalities. However, these numbers could be underestimated given the difficulties in getting reliable data on dormitories, in particular due to their complicated ownership structures. These facilities frequently provide housing to migrant workers and marginalised population groups, such as the Roma, who are often excluded from regular housing markets. According to a survey by the Ivan Gabal Sociological

Institute, first carried out in 2006 and more recently in 2015, the Roma community represents about half of the people living in so-called "socially excluded localities", i.e. locations with more than 20% of people living in inadequate conditions (indicated by the number of recipients of the living allowance) and inhabiting a physically or symbolically delimited space (Čada et al., 2015[53]).

In addition to people living in substandard conditions or inadequate housing, there are also a number of people who are either homeless or at risk of becoming homeless. According to the Ministry of Labour and Social Affairs, in 2016, there were around 68 500 homeless people (of which 21 230 adults and 2 600 minors are "roofless", according to the 2019 census) and 119 000 are at the risk of becoming homeless across the Czech Republic.

Conclusion

With house prices rising sharply in the Czech Republic over the past few years and much faster than household incomes, many Czech households have been struggling to access the housing market in cities, especially newcomers who do not own their dwelling. The private rental market has also offered few viable alternative affordable housing options in cities. Furthermore, living in cities imposes a heavy financial burden on Czech households, mainly because of housing-related expenditure such as those related to electricity, gas and other fuels. The increase in house prices and rents in Czech cities has been explained by the mismatch between strong demand for housing and an insufficient increase in housing supply. Even when housing supply has increased, it has not in the municipalities where it is most needed, i.e. those where housing demand is the highest. Improving housing affordability in cities in the Czech Republic will require national, regional and local action to steer housing development to urban areas where this is most needed and to expand more affordable rental housing, among other actions (see Chapter 2).

References

Bétin, M. and V. Ziemann (2019), "How responsive are housing markets in the OECD? Regional level estimates", *OECD Economics Department Working Papers*, No. 1590, OECD Publishing, Paris, https://dx.doi.org/10.1787/1342258c-en. [45]

Čada, K. et al. (2015), *Analysis of Socially Excluded Localities in the Czech Republic*, GAC, Prague, https://www.ohchr.org/Documents/Issues/Housing/InformalSettlements/PublicDefenderCzechRepublic_2.pdf. [53]

Cavalleri, M., B. Cournède and E. Özsöğüt (2019), "How responsive are housing markets in the OECD? National level estimates", *OECD Economics Department Working Papers*, No. 1589, OECD Publishing, Paris, https://dx.doi.org/10.1787/4777e29a-en. [46]

Cavalleri, M., B. Cournède and V. Ziemann (2019), "Housing markets and macroeconomic risks", *OECD Economics Department Working Papers*, No. 1555, OECD Publishing, Paris, https://dx.doi.org/10.1787/737133d8-en. [35]

City of Prague (n.d.), *Prague Transportation Yearbook*, Various years. [41]

CNB (2020), *Czech National Bank Statistics*, Czech National Bank, https://www.cnb.cz/en/statistics/. [28]

CNB (2020), *Financial Stability Report 2019/2020*, Czech National Bank, https://www.cnb.cz/export/sites/cnb/en/financial-stability/.galleries/fs_reports/fsr_2019-2020/fsr_2019-2020.pdf. [11]

CNB (2019), *Financial Stability Report 2018/2019*, Czech National Bank, https://www.cnb.cz/export/sites/cnb/en/financial-stability/.galleries/fs_reports/fsr_2018-2019/fsr_2018-2019.pdf. [27]

CNB (2018), *Financial Stability Report 2017/2018*, Czech National Bank, https://www.cnb.cz/export/sites/cnb/en/financial-stability/.galleries/fs_reports/fsr_2017-2018/fsr_2017-2018.pdf. [25]

Czech Statistical Office (2020), *Czech Statistical Office Statistics*, https://www.czso.cz/csu/czso/statistics. [16]

Czech Statistical Office (n.d.), *Statistical Yearbook of Prague*. [40]

de Boer, R. and R. Bitetti (2014), "A Revival of the Private Rental Sector of the Housing Market?: Lessons from Germany, Finland, the Czech Republic and the Netherlands", *OECD Economics Department Working Papers*, No. 1170, OECD Publishing, Paris, https://dx.doi.org/10.1787/5jxv9f32j0zp-en. [9]

Deloitte (2020), *Deloitte Real Index Q1 2020: Actual Prices of Apartments Sold in the Czech Republic*, https://www2.deloitte.com/content/dam/Deloitte/cz/Documents/real-estate/EN-Real-index-1Q-2020.pdf. [17]

Deloitte (2020), *Property Index: Overview of European Residential Markets*. [15]

Deloitte (2019), *Prague Hospitality Report. Tourism, Hotels and P2P Accommodation*. [37]

Dijkstra, L., H. Poelman and P. Veneri (2019), "The EU-OECD definition of a functional urban area", *OECD Regional Development Working Papers*, No. 2019/11, OECD Publishing, Paris, https://dx.doi.org/10.1787/d58cb34d-en. [32]

Dumont, A. (2019), *Housing Affordability in the US: Trends by Geography, Tenure, and Household Income*, Board of Governors of the Federal Reserve System, Washington, https://doi.org/10.17016/2380-7172.2430. [5]

EC (2020), *Country Report Czechia 2020: 2020 European Semester: Assessment of Progress on Structural Reforms, Prevention and Correction of Macroeconomic Imbalances, and Results of In-depth Reviews under Regulation (EU) No 1176/2011*, European Commission, https://eur-lex.europa.eu/legal-content/EN/TXT/PDF/?uri=CELEX:52020SC0502&from=EN. [13]

EC (2018), *European Construction Sector Observatory: Country Profile Czech Republic*, European Commission. [43]

EU Energy Poverty Observatory (2020), *Member State Report: Czech Republic*, https://www.energypoverty.eu/sites/default/files/downloads/observatory-documents/20-06/extended_member_state_report_-_czechia.pdf. [49]

Euromonitor International (2019), *Top 100 City Destinations. 2019 Edition*. [36]

European Central Bank (2020), *Statistical Data Warehouse*, https://sdw.ecb.europa.eu/home.do. [29]

European Commission (2010), *COMMUNICATION FROM THE COMMISSION TO THE EUROPEAN PARLIAMENT, THE COUNCIL, THE EUROPEAN ECONOMIC AND SOCIAL COMMITTEE AND THE COMMITTEE OF THE REGIONS: The European Platform against Poverty and Social Exclusion: A European framework for social and territorial cohesion*, European Commission, Brussels, https://eur-lex.europa.eu/LexUriServ/LexUriServ.do?uri=COM%3A2010%3A0758%3AFIN%3AEN%3APDF. [2]

Eurostat (2020), *Eurostat Income and Living Conditions*, https://ec.europa.eu/eurostat/web/income-and-living-conditions/data/database. [48]

Eurostat (n.d.), *Housing Statistics: Statistics Explained.* [3]

Francke, M. and M. Korevaar (2021), "Housing markets in a pandemic: Evidence from historical outbreaks", *SSRN Electronic Journal*, http://dx.doi.org/10.2139/ssrn.3566909. [20]

IEA (n.d.), *IEA Data and Statistics*, https://www.iea.org/data-and-statistics/charts/energy-intensity-per-floor-area-of-residential-space-heating-in-selected-iea-countries-2000-2018. [52]

IMF (2018), *2018 Article IV Consultation: Czech Republic*, International Monetary Fund. [33]

Lux, M. and M. Mikeszova (2012), "Property restitution and private rental housing in transition: The case of the Czech Republic", *Housing Studies*, Vol. 27/1, pp. 77-96, http://dx.doi.org/10.1080/02673037.2012.629643. [8]

Lux, M. and P. Sunega (2017), "Social housing in the Czech Republic: The change of a trend?", *Critical Housing Analysis*, Vol. 4/1, pp. 81-89, http://dx.doi.org/10.13060/23362839.2017.4.1.327. [10]

Lux, M. and P. Sunega (2010), "Private rental housing in the Czech Republic: Growth and ...?", *Czech Sociological Review*, Vol. 46/3. [7]

OECD (2021), *Analytical House Price Indicators*, https://stats.oecd.org/. [12]

OECD (2021), "Housing overcrowding", (indicator), https://dx.doi.org/10.1787/96953cb4-en. [50]

OECD (2020), *Affordable Housing Database*, OECD, Paris, http://oe.cd/ahd. [6]

OECD (2020), *Income Distribution Database*, https://stats.oecd.org/. [23]

OECD (2020), "Mitigating the impact of COVID-19 on tourism and supporting recovery", *OECD Tourism Papers*, No. 2020/03, OECD Publishing, Paris, https://dx.doi.org/10.1787/47045bae-en. [18]

OECD (2020), *OECD Economic Outlook, Volume 2020 Issue 1*, OECD Publishing, Paris, https://dx.doi.org/10.1787/0d1d1e2e-en. [24]

OECD (2020), *OECD Economic Surveys: Czech Republic 2020*, OECD Publishing, Paris, https://dx.doi.org/10.1787/1b180a5a-en. [21]

OECD (2020), *Population Statistics*, https://stats.oecd.org/. [30]

OECD (2020), *Productivity Database*, https://stats.oecd.org/. [22]

OECD (2020), "The territorial impact of COVID-19: Managing the crisis across levels of government", *OECD Policy Responses to Coronavirus (COVID-19)*, OECD, Paris, http://www.oecd.org/coronavirus/policy-responses/the-territorial-impact-of-covid-19-managing-the-crisis-across-levels-of-government-d3e314e1/#section-d1e182. [19]

OECD (2019), *Under Pressure: The Squeezed Middle Class*, OECD Publishing, Paris, https://dx.doi.org/10.1787/689afed1-en. [14]

OECD (2018), *OECD Economic Surveys: Czech Republic 2018*, OECD Publishing, Paris, https://dx.doi.org/10.1787/eco_surveys-cze-2018-en. [26]

OECD (2018), *OECD Environmental Performance Reviews: Czech Republic 2018*, OECD Environmental Performance Reviews, OECD Publishing, Paris, https://dx.doi.org/10.1787/9789264300958-en. [39]

OECD (2018), *Rethinking Urban Sprawl: Moving Towards Sustainable Cities*, OECD Publishing, Paris, https://dx.doi.org/10.1787/9789264189881-en. [38]

OECD (n.d.), *National Accounts database*, https://stats.oecd.org/. [47]

OECD/EC (2020), *Cities in the World: A New Perspective on Urbanisation*, OECD Urban Studies, OECD Publishing, Paris, https://dx.doi.org/10.1787/d0efcbda-en. [31]

OECD/MMR (2020), *OECD-MMR Housing Survey of Municipalities in the Czech Republic*. [42]

Office for National Statistics (2020), *Housing Affordability in England and Wales: 2019*. [4]

Office of the Government (2019), *2019 European Semester: National Reform Programme of the Czech Republic 2019*, https://ec.europa.eu/info/sites/info/files/2019-european-semester-national-reform-programme-czech-republic_en.pdf. [51]

PwC/Urban Land Institute (2017), *Emerging Trends in Real Estate: Europe 2018*, PwC and the Urban Land Institute, London. [34]

UN (2018), "Metadata Indicator 11.1.1: Proportion of urban population living in slums, informal settlements or inadequate housing", United Nations, https://unstats.un.org/sdgs/metadata/files/Metadata-11-01-01.pdf. [1]

World Bank (2019), *Doing Business 2020*, World Bank, Washington, DC. [44]

Note

[1] For more detailed information on the OECD methodology defining FUAs, please see Dijkstra, Poelman and Veneri (2019[32]).

2 Policies for housing affordability in cities in the Czech Republic

With the economic and social fallout from the COVID-19 crisis continuing to unfold, both local and national governments have to enact longer-term changes to the housing market to ensure housing affordability. The Czech Republic must brace itself for further demand for affordable housing, and act swiftly to keep housing affordable for its population, particularly in cities. The national government can guide and harmonise social housing provision by municipalities, help provide housing to the most vulnerable members of society and reduce substandard housing in cities. However, housing affordability must also be addressed more broadly, by increasing access to the private rental market and encouraging housing development in municipalities where demand is high. Joint planning across municipalities, aligning housing affordability objectives with other social and environmental objectives and deploying spatial and land use planning instruments strategically can also be powerful tools to make housing more affordable in cities.

Introduction

While providing affordable housing constitutes a challenge for the Czech Republic overall, it is particularly urgent in cities, which are confronted with a faster increase in house prices than the rest of the country due to continuously rising housing demand and structural constraints on housing supply (see Chapter 1). Furthermore, high housing prices in cities can lead to urban sprawl by pricing residents out of city centres. Poor housing conditions in cities also undermine people's wellbeing and health outcomes and reduce energy efficiency in buildings, further undermining housing affordability. Making housing more affordable in cities goes beyond providing urban residents with basic shelter: it contributes to achieving broader national and local economic, social and environmental policy objectives. With better access to affordable housing, people are more likely to be able to participate in the economy to their full potential, upgrade their skills, socialise and engage in civic and political life.

Against the backdrop of the COVID-19 pandemic, the Czech Republic has taken a number of emergency measures related to housing, including instituting a mortgage forbearance, one of the most common support measures across OECD countries (OECD, 2021[1]). Beyond such emergency measures and although the full effects of the COVID-19 crisis on housing affordability remain to be seen, the pandemic has renewed concerns around pre-existing challenges such as gaps in housing quality and access to services, and increased housing insecurity for many households (OECD, 2021[1]). With some emergency measures becoming long-term as uncertainty about the length of the crisis and the extent of the social and economic fallout continues, both local and national governments also have to enact longer-term changes to the housing market to ensure housing affordability.

To alleviate the housing affordability challenge in cities beyond the COVID-19 crisis, national and local governments in the Czech Republic can implement both direct and indirect policy instruments. Direct instruments target housing affordability specifically, for example by providing social housing and allocating housing benefits. Indirect policies can also affect housing supply and housing affordability, for example through building regulations, land use and spatial planning. The impact of both types of policies must be carefully assessed from an early stage of policy design to avoid unintended outcomes on housing affordability.

This chapter will assess the current housing policy framework affecting cities in the Czech Republic, identify potential gaps and offer policy recommendations to improve policy effectiveness.[1] First, the chapter will analyse direct housing policy instruments at the national and local levels that can affect housing affordability in cities. Second, it will explore indirect policy instruments such as spatial and land use planning, building regulations, co-ordination between sectoral policies and municipalities, and subnational government finance. In each section, the chapter will propose a set of policy recommendations for national and local governments.

Box 2.1. Olomouc and Pilsen (Plzeň): Mid-sized cities exhibiting several trends and challenges related to housing affordability in cities in the Czech Republic

Throughout this chapter, several of the main challenges and issues in housing policies of Czech cities will also be explored through the cases of the cities of Olomouc and Pilsen.

With a population of around 171 700 inhabitants, Pilsen is a city in the west of the Czech Republic and the capital of the Pilsen Region. It is one of the most expensive cities in the Czech Republic with an average price of purchased flats of around CZK 45 000 per square metre (EUR 1 730/m^2) – 1.5 to 2 times higher than neighbouring municipalities – with prices of small housing units in the most expensive areas of the city climbing to CZK 65 000 per m^2 (EUR 2 500/m^2). One of the main challenges related to housing affordability in Pilsen is the housing cost overburden experienced by many households, in particular low-income households (e.g. single-parent families, families with unemployed members) and single-person households, including mainly senior citizens, mainly due to high energy and maintenance costs (accounting for half of the total housing costs). Households that are particularly vulnerable to loss of housing include people who have just started or ended their professional careers, single parents (most frequently women), people disadvantaged on the housing market due to their nationality, race or religion, adolescents and young people leaving institutionalised care or foster care, ex-prisoners, senior citizens, disabled persons, homeless people and low-income households.

With a population of 100 400 inhabitants, Olomouc is the sixth-largest city in the Czech Republic, capital of the Olomouc Region located in the east of the Czech Republic and home to a large student population. House prices in Olomouc are also among the most expensive in the country, with new dwellings ranging from CZK 45 000 to CZK 65 000 per m². This is higher than prices in neighbouring municipalities where the housing stock is mostly made up of houses, although prices for newly completed family houses in municipalities that are close and well connected to Olomouc are almost as high. This increase has mostly been driven by demand substantially exceeding supply, even though housing supply has been increasing faster than the national average. High demand has partly been the result of the large population of students and teachers of Palacký University, contributing to rising prices, especially on the rental market. Approximately 5 000 students are living in university dormitories and at least 5 000 students in rented flats in Olomouc. As the city of Olomouc owns only around 3% of the city's housing stock, the municipality has a limited influence on the availability of housing. Finally, Olomouc has found that some private landlords engage in discriminatory practices and may turn down the Roma community, for example, or those receiving a housing allowance, old-age pensioners or families with children.

Source: Information provided by the cities of Olomouc and Pilsen.

National and local governments in the Czech Republic can influence housing affordability in cities through a range of direct policy instruments

The Housing Strategy provides a dedicated national framework for housing affordability policy in the Czech Republic

In 2010, the Czech Ministry of Regional Development (MMR) produced a national urban policy called the "Principles of Urban Policy" (*Zásady Urbánní Politiky*). This framework document provides guidance to co-ordinate urban development activities at all levels of government and links existing sectoral policies with urban policies. It contains six principles covering the regional nature of urban policy, the polycentric development of population patterns, the development of towns as development poles in a territory and care for the urban environment, including mitigation and adaptation to climate change and the protection of green spaces and green belts (OECD/UN-Habitat, 2018[2]). Written by the same ministry, the Czech Republic has a specific national housing policy in place, called the *Housing Policy Strategy in the Czech Republic Till 2020* (hereinafter the Housing Strategy). The Housing Strategy focuses on three priorities: i) affordability of adequate housing; ii) stability of the housing market; and iii) quality of housing (MMR, 2011[3]). This framework offers a comprehensive outline of the policy instruments available in the Czech Republic, which are summarised in Table 2.1, according to the categorisation of housing policy instruments across OECD countries (Box 2.2). Initially established in 2011 and set to be renewed in 2021, it follows a clear time horizon and is updated on a regular basis to keep abreast of new trends and developments on the housing market. Furthermore, its focus on housing quality as well as quantity constitutes an important effort to adopt a holistic approach to housing affordability, especially as the housing stock in Czech cities is often old and in need of energy efficiency improvements (see Chapter 1).

Table 2.1. Main housing policy instruments in the Czech Republic

Support for homebuyers and homeowners	Subsidies to households to facilitate homeownership	• Homeownership programme (*Program Vlastní bydlení*) loan scheme for the purchase or construction of dwellings for young people up to 40 years of age and with a child under 15 years of age. Government Decree No. 1/2021 Coll. • Subsidies for loans for young families for the acquisition of housing (birth of a child) under different programmes.
	Subsidised mortgages and guarantees to homebuyers	
	Tax relief for access to homeownership	• Tax relief for mortgage payments (*Nezdanitelná cást základu dane*)
	Support to finance housing regeneration	• Homeownership programme (*Program Vlastní bydlení*) loan scheme for the regeneration of dwellings for young people up to 40 years of age and with a child under 15 years of age. Government Decree No. 1/2021 Coll. • Building retrofit subsidies: PANEL 2013+ programme – the programme provides low-interest loans for the renovation of multi-dwelling buildings. • Housing flats without barriers: MMR support given to owners of multi-unit buildings to improve the housing stock through barrier-free access. • Programme for the regeneration of public areas in housing estates: Programme according to Government Decree No. 390/2017 Coll. allows municipalities to finance the regeneration of public areas of housing estates through subsidies or subsidies and loans. • Insulation: Interest-free loan for energy modernisation of multi-unit buildings (Government Decree No. 16/2020 Coll.). • Loan Programme for the Reconstruction of Dwellings Affected by a Natural Disaster governed by Government Decree No. 319/2014 Coll.
Support for homeowners and renters	Housing allowances	• Housing allowance (*Príspevek na bydlení*): For both rental and housing costs. • Housing supplement (*Doplatek na bydlení*): For social assistance recipients (families and individuals in material need). Can be granted in addition to the housing allowance for households that are still unable to cover their basic necessities.
	Subsidies for the development of affordable rental housing (other than social housing)	• Rental housing development programme: Loans to support the construction or reconstruction of rental housing for defined population groups, i.e. seniors (over 65), disabled or limited-income citizens, victims of a natural disaster or young people under 30 years of age. Government Decree No. 284/2011 Coll. • Construction for municipalities: For the acquisition of affordable and social housing, social houses and mixed houses – Loans for affordable flats and subsidies for social flats. Government Decree No. 112/2019 Coll.

Source: OECD (2019[4]) and Ministry of Regional Development (MMR, 2018[5]).

Box 2.2. Housing affordability instruments across the OECD

Support for homeownership and homeowners

- *Subsidies to homebuyers to facilitate home ownership*: These measures include one-off grants for the purchase of a residential dwelling, covering part or all of the value of the dwelling. They are often reserved for first-time homebuyers with income levels below a given threshold who purchase dwellings with certain characteristics.
- *Subsidised mortgages and mortgage guarantees for homebuyers*: Subsidised mortgages provided by or subsidised by the government, for the purchase of a residential dwelling; measures can also consist of down payment assistance or mortgage guarantees provided by the government.

- *Mortgage relief for over-indebted homeowners*: Subsidies and measures to avoid foreclosure on residential dwellings that are owned by households in financial distress. These include subsidies for mortgage payments and payment of arrears, postponement of payments, refinancing mortgages and mortgage-to-rent schemes.
- *Tax relief for homeowners*: Tax deductions or tax credits granted to individual taxpayers for the purchase of their main residence. These may include tax relief measures such as mortgage tax relief or tax relief to first-time homebuyers for the costs (e.g. legal fees, disbursements and land transfer taxes) associated with the purchase of a home.
- *Support to finance housing regeneration*: Tax deductions, tax credits and/or grants to finance the regeneration of existing residential dwellings (e.g. energy efficiency improvements, quality upgrades, etc.).

Support for homeowners and tenants

- *Housing allowances*: Recurrent means-tested income transfers to households paid to either owners or tenants towards their housing costs. Housing allowances can include rent, payment of mortgage and/or interest, utilities, insurance and services.
- *Subsidies to develop affordable housing*: Measures providing grants, tax relief or subsidised land to developers to finance the development of new affordable housing. Such measures may also include rental housing, "shared ownership" and "rent-to-buy" schemes.

Support for the rental market

- *Social rental housing*: Residential rental accommodation provided at submarket prices and allocated according to specific rules rather than according to market mechanisms. Programmes in this area can cover construction, regeneration, management, maintenance and financing of social rental housing.
- *Tax relief measures for rental costs*: Tax deductions or tax credits to individual taxpayers for rental housing-related expenditures in the market rental sector. Tax relief measures may aim to benefit tenants and/or owners/landlords of rental dwellings.
- *Rent guarantees and deposits*: Publicly provided guarantees on rents or deposits in the market rental sector.
- *Rent controls or ceilings*: Restrictions on initial rent levels and/or rent level increases (for sitting tenants and/or new tenants) in the private rental market.
- *Minimum quality regulations for rental dwellings*: Legal requirements to ensure a minimum level of quality of dwellings available for rent; these may include, for instance, minimum requirements relating to safety, health and maintenance.
- *Measures to regulate short-term holiday rentals*: Measures vary but may include restrictions on the number of days that a holiday rental property can be leased over the course of a year; the mandatory presence of hosts on the property during the stay; the imposition of taxes and/or fees for such properties, etc.

Source: OECD (2019[4]), *OECD Affordable Housing Database*, OECD, Paris.

Despite the existence of this concrete national housing policy framework, some limitations are hampering its effective implementation. An example of such limitations is the lack of legal definitions for important terms such as "social housing". The lack of a national legislative framework for social housing has led to an "underregulated" (de Boer and Bitetti, 2014[6]) and inefficient social housing sector, which leaves some uncertainty in the application of the overall housing policy framework.

The national housing policy framework is also complicated by the number of actors within the system, which requires an effective mechanism to align goals, resources and programmes. At the national level, housing policy is primarily led by the MMR. However, other ministries administer certain housing benefits and related programmes without clear co-ordination mechanisms. For example, prominent actors include the Ministry of Labour and Social Affairs (social security allowance for housing, contribution for renovations of disabled people), the Ministry of Finance (building savings scheme, tax relief measures), the Ministry of the Environment (energy renovations scheme) and the Ministry of the Interior (integration of asylum seekers). At the local level, municipalities are responsible for housing provision, including affordable and social housing. They also have competency over grant allocation and distribution, urban planning and zoning.

Box 2.3. Pilsen: The first Czech city with a strategy dedicated to social and affordable housing

The municipal council of the city of Pilsen approved a new Strategic Plan for the City of Pilsen in 2018, which includes a section on housing. In addition to the strategic plan, which represents an important decision-making tool for the city, Pilsen is the first city in the Czech Republic that introduced a Strategy of Social and Affordable Housing, which covers the period of 2019-22. The strategy analyses the housing situation in Pilsen, with a focus on households that are unable to get standard rental housing under market conditions, and proposes measures to resolve the issue. The strategy introduced several objectives, including to:

- Propose solutions for selected groups according to their housing needs by 2022 by increasing the capacity of individual housing by at least 150 flats, by raising the capacity of special-purpose flats and wheelchair-accessible flats and by strengthening the system of shelters and the scope of the city surveillance system.
- Ensure that applicants for municipal housing are able to access a flat under fully transparent conditions and within a reasonable time period, i.e. within six months of submitting their application.

Based on its analysis of social housing applications and demographic trends, the strategy focuses on four target groups: senior citizens, people with disabilities, young households under 35 years of age and social workers.

Pilsen's housing strategy aims to increase the accessibility of housing by improving access of selected vulnerable groups to affordable housing. In addition to this type of direct instrument, better use of land use and zoning plans as well as greater co-ordination with surrounding municipalities to facilitate the integration of housing and transport could alleviate pressure on Pilsen's housing market.

Another obstacle is a lack of financial resources, both at the national and local levels. The government's spending to support housing affordability in the Czech Republic is generally low compared to other OECD countries. In 2017, state expenditure on housing was only 0.39% of gross domestic product (GDP) (MMR, 2018[5]). This includes about 0.18% of GDP spent on housing allowances (see below) and 0.01% of GDP on supporting social rental housing (OECD, 2021[7]), compared to 0.34% in New Zealand and 0.21% in Belgium (OECD, 2021[7]).

Housing allowances provide important support to many Czech urban households but are not fully taken up

Two main housing policy instruments in the Czech Republic are the housing allowance (paid to about 200 000 recipients) and the housing supplement (paid to about 50 000 lowest-income households), which are both distributed by the Ministry of Labour and Social Affairs. The Czech Republic spends about 0.18% of its GDP on social housing allowances, which is however below the OECD average of 0.25% (Figure 2.1).

The housing allowance (*příspěvek na bydlení*) targets low-income families and individuals who cannot afford housing at market prices. The housing allowance is conditional on housing costs exceeding 30% of the household's "decisive" income (or 35% in Prague).[2] Recipients must also be registered as permanent residents to be eligible for the housing allowance (EC, n.d.[8]). The allowance is paid through a cash transfer to eligible households without conditions of tenure, i.e. it is available to private tenants, social tenants as well as owner-occupants. Normative housing costs, used to determine eligibility for the housing allowance, are calculated as the average total cost of housing according to the size of the municipality and the number of household members. They include rent, comparable costs and prices of services and energy. They are calculated on the average consumption of services and energy and the appropriate size of dwellings for a given number of people permanently living in them. About two-thirds of housing allowance recipients were private renters in 2017 (OECD, 2019[9]). However, unawareness of the benefit, the complicated administrative process to receive it and adjustments to the formula determining the income taken into account to assess eligibility resulting in more complexity, could lead to some "non-uptake" of the housing allowance among eligible households.

The housing supplement (*doplatek na bydlení*) provides additional financial assistance to low-income households. Despite its name, the housing supplement is a general transfer to low-income households that is actually independent of housing expenditure. Although the average amount of the housing supplement has increased in recent years (reaching an average of CZK 4 128 per month in 2020), the number of households receiving the supplement has decreased to an average of 32 800 households per month in 2020.

Figure 2.1. Public spending on housing allowances, OECD countries

Government spending as % of GDP, 2018 or latest available year

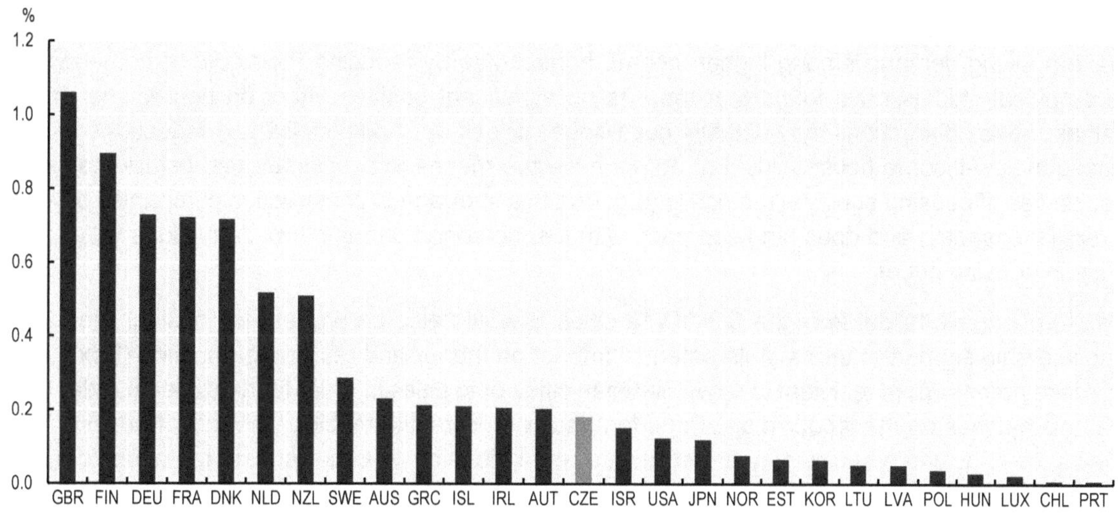

Note: Data for 2018 refer to the responses to the 2019 OECD Questionnaire on Affordable and Social Housing, except for Hungary, Ireland, Japan and Korea where they refer to 2016 QuAsh, i.e. around 2015.
Source: OECD (2019[4]), *OECD Affordable Housing Database*, OECD, Paris.

When they are well-targeted, housing allowances have been found to enhance equality in access to housing and constitute an important housing affordability policy instrument in many OECD countries. However, housing allowances can be passed through to housing prices in areas where housing supply is limited. Evidence in France and the United Kingdom, for example, shows that a large share of housing allowances are captured by landlords, who raise rents by 78% and 50% respectively (Gibbons and Manning, 2006[10]; Fack, 2006[11]). Thus, it is important to combine them with other policies to increase the supply of low-income housing.

The Czech Republic is planning to merge the housing allowance and supplement. Simplifying the complex housing allowance system to allow more people to access the benefits they are entitled to would be a positive step in theory but only if the most vulnerable households (such as those living in temporary accommodation, including "dormitories") are eligible.

While several policy instruments aim at facilitating access to homeownership in cities, their potential downside needs to be taken into account

Owner-occupied housing is the dominant type of tenure in the Czech Republic. Multiple policy instruments are therefore used to encourage homeownership, mostly via demand-side subsidies, including grants and tax relief, buy-to-rent schemes and relief for distressed mortgages.

Several programmes run by the State Investment Support Fund (SISF, formerly State Housing Development Fund) target specific groups who might face obstacles to homeownership. For example, the homeownership programme (*Program Vlastní bydlení*) is a loan scheme for the regeneration of dwellings for young people up to 40 years of age and with a child under 15 years of age. In 2017, the precursors to these programmes helped finance more than 2 000 flats (Sirovátka, Jahoda and Malý, 2019[12]), which represents only a very small percentage of households in the Czech Republic. Additionally, tax incentives to support home ownership mainly take the form of the deduction of mortgage interest payments from the personal income tax (PIT) base and they are estimated to be the largest housing support programme in the Czech Republic (Sirovátka, Jahoda and Malý, 2019[12]). Despite a reduction in the maximum mortgage interest payment deduction in 2021, 2020 saw the abolition of the real estate acquisition tax of 4% of the acquisition value, creating an incentive for homeownership.

However, support for homeownership may not be enough to solve the affordability issue for low-income families for whom house prices are too high to be able to purchase a dwelling. Furthermore, some policies to encourage homeownership may in fact be counterproductive. For example, mortgage interest tax deductions for homeownership may disproportionately benefit high-income households. They usually increase housing demand among higher-income households by reducing their cost of homeownership, while empirical studies have found that there is no significant positive effect on homeownership rates overall as the tax deductions may actually push house prices up. Additionally, tax deductions cannot be accessed by low-income households that do not have the means to access the real estate market, even with subsidies. If housing supply is restrictive (e.g. due to a shortage of construction companies or workers, land regulations, etc.) and does not keep pace with the increased demand, tax deductions will likely lead to a rise in housing prices.

Given the economic fallout from the COVID-19 crisis, it would also be prudent to consider the effects of homeownership support in terms of its potential impact on labour and residential mobility (Box 2.4), as it could make homeowners reluctant to move between cities or to cities in order to take jobs. In order to avoid spatial mismatches on the labour market due to a lack of residential mobility, the mix of housing tenures in cities should include a sufficient share of private rental housing. A larger private rental sector can help promote residential mobility, increase housing options for households and generate a competitive supply and thus affordable prices, and should therefore be encouraged. In addition to expanding the private rental sector, reducing barriers to a more responsive housing supply through land use and planning instruments could also facilitate residential mobility (see the following section on indirect housing policy instruments).

Box 2.4. Advantages and disadvantages of homeownership

Policies affecting the owner-occupied housing market can increase access to homeownership and alleviate the housing cost burden for homebuyers. Support for homeownership can be motivated by several economic and social benefits that are associated with homeownership. In addition to being a vehicle for wealth accumulation, extensive literature has found homeownership to be correlated to benefits such as:

- Better educational attainments for children (Boehm and Schlottmann, 1999[13]).
- More commitment and community engagement by owners compared to renters and less crime (DiPasquale and Glaeser, 1999[14]).
- Better physical and mental health of homeowners (Macintyre et al., 1998[15]).
- Increased life satisfaction (Lam, 1985[16]).

However, homeownership also has disadvantages. First, it can hinder labour mobility and be a driver of structural rigidities. As transaction costs associated with the purchase or sale of property are high, homeowners tend to be less mobile (Causa and Pichelmann, 2020[17]). Although this lack of mobility in comparison to tenants is the basis for some of the benefits of homeownership (as it is seen to engender greater commitment to the community), it also makes it harder for homeowners to move. This can be a problem when there is a rise in unemployment or an economic crisis and homeowners are reluctant to move (Oswald, 1996[18]). Some economists maintain that homeownership and the resulting lack of mobility may ultimately make economic crises even worse in the future (Burchardt and Hills, 1998[19]). In the Czech Republic, the post-socialist privatisation of public housing has led to a strong cultural preference for homeownership, with Lux and Sunega arguing that some Czech homeowners are willing to suffer the inherent costs of homeownership in order to maintain occupancy of their current residence (2012[20]). This phenomenon is referred to as a "satisfaction paradox" where homeownership increases life satisfaction regardless of the actual level of poverty (Rohe and Stegman, 1994[21]).

Source: Boehm, T. and A. Schlottmann (1999[13]), "Does home ownership by parents have an economic impact on their children?", https://ideas.repec.org/a/eee/jhouse/v8y1999i3p217-232.html (accessed on 26 February 2021); DiPasquale, D. and E. Glaeser (1999[14]), "Incentives and social capital: Are homeowners better citizens?", https://www.sciencedirect.com/science/article/pii/S0094119098920988 (accessed on 26 February 2021); Macintyre, S. et al. (1998[15]), "Do housing tenure and car access predict health because they are simply markers of income or self esteem? A Scottish study", http://dx.doi.org/10.1136/jech.52.10.657; Lam, J. (1985[16]), "Type of structure, satisfaction and propensity to move", http://dx.doi.org/10.1080/08882746.1985.11429958; Causa, O. and J. Pichelmann (2020[17]), "Should I stay or should I go? Housing and residential mobility across OECD countries", https://doi.org/10.1787/d91329c2-en (accessed on 26 February 2021); Oswald, A. (1996[18]), *A Conjecture on the Explanation for High Unemployment in the Industrialized Nations: Part I*, https://ageconsearch.umn.edu/record/268744/ (accessed on 26 February 2021); Burchardt, T. and J. Hills (1998[19]), "From public to private: The case of mortgage payment insurance in Great Britain", http://dx.doi.org/10.1080/02673039883308; Lux, M. and P. Sunega (2012[20]), "Labour mobility and housing", https://EconPapers.repec.org/RePEc:sae:urbstu:v:49:y:2012:i:3:p:489-504 (accessed on 26 February 2021); Rohe, W. and M. Stegman (1994[21]), "The effects of homeownership: On the self-esteem, perceived control and life satisfaction of low-income people", http://dx.doi.org/10.1080/01944369408975571.

The social housing segment varies across municipalities but generally remains small and underregulated

In the Czech Republic, social housing is understood as municipally owned housing that is allocated based on criteria decided by the municipality. A national framework exists in the form of the *Social Housing Policy Strategy of the Czech Republic 2015-2025*, approved by the Czech government in 2015 and under the responsibility of both the MMR and the Ministry of Labour and Social Affairs. However, it does not constitute legislation on social housing and the term "social housing" remains used in different ways throughout official documents. There is also no clear and systematic connection between the Social Housing Policy Strategy and the aforementioned Housing Strategy.

The Social Housing Policy Strategy covers three types of housing, depending on the degree of housing deprivation:

- "Crisis" housing, which is temporary and emergency housing solutions for households whose housing situation needs to be solved urgently, with compulsory co-operation with social workers.
- "Social" housing for families and people without a roof, for a minimum of two years and compulsory co-operation with **social workers.**
- "Affordable" housing for a minimum of two years involving voluntary co-operation with social workers.

The Social Housing Policy Strategy identifies the most prominent social housing challenges (including the high financial burden created by housing expenses for some households, discrimination of specific groups of people in terms of access to affordable housing, inconsistency of interpretations and the current conditions of social housing in municipalities in the Czech Republic). It also outlines the objectives to be reached by the Czech government by 2025 – including the adoption of the law on social housing.

The Social Housing Policy Strategy also aims to guide government action and is therefore considered binding for ministries. However, it does not constitute a formal piece of legislation and the actual providers of social housing, i.e. municipalities, are not bound by the strategy, which can impede its implementation.

The social housing stock in the Czech Republic is too small to meet the demand of all low-income and vulnerable households

As discussed in Chapter 1, the municipal rental sector was created after 1991 by transferring state-owned dwellings to municipalities. Municipalities then privatised a major part of their housing stock, often because they lacked financial and human resources to ensure the maintenance. According to the OECD Affordable Housing Database, social rental dwellings account for only 0.4% of the total number of dwellings in the Czech Republic (OECD, 2020[22]) – a very low share compared with other OECD countries (e.g. 37.7% in the Netherlands, 20% in Austria, 7.6% in Poland, 4.0% in Hungary) (Figure 2.2). However, this very low share is potentially the consequence of an unclear definition of what constitutes social housing in the Czech Republic. Even after excluding outliers, municipalities participating in the OECD-MMR housing survey indicated that they own 8.7% of their total housing stock and provide it to residents at below-market rates.[3]

According to the OECD-MMR housing survey, more than half of the municipalities covered by the survey own housing (57%). However, this percentage varies significantly according to the size of the municipality, ranging from less than 40% among very small municipalities to close to 90% of large municipalities (Figure 2.3). Furthermore, more than 90% of municipalities that own housing make at least part of their housing stock available as social housing and 73% provide their entire housing stock at below-market rents. In the average Czech municipality that provides social housing,[4] the share of social housing units within the total housing stock is 4.4%, which is equivalent to 335 units per 10 000 inhabitants. Larger municipalities tend to provide significantly more social housing. On average, if the municipal population size doubles, the share of social housing within the housing stock increases by 1 percentage point.

Figure 2.2. Size of the social rental housing stock

Number of social rental dwellings as a share of total number of dwellings

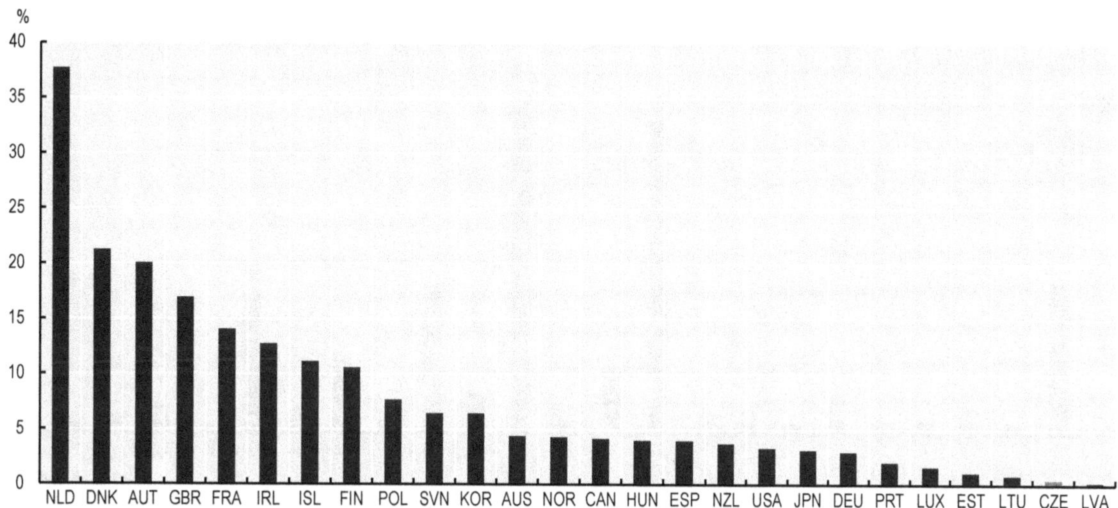

Note: Data are for 2018 or for latest year available. Data for the Czech Republic are from the latest census undertaken in 2011.
Source: OECD (2019[4]), *OECD Affordable Housing Database*, OECD, Paris.

Figure 2.3. Percentage of municipalities that own housing by population size

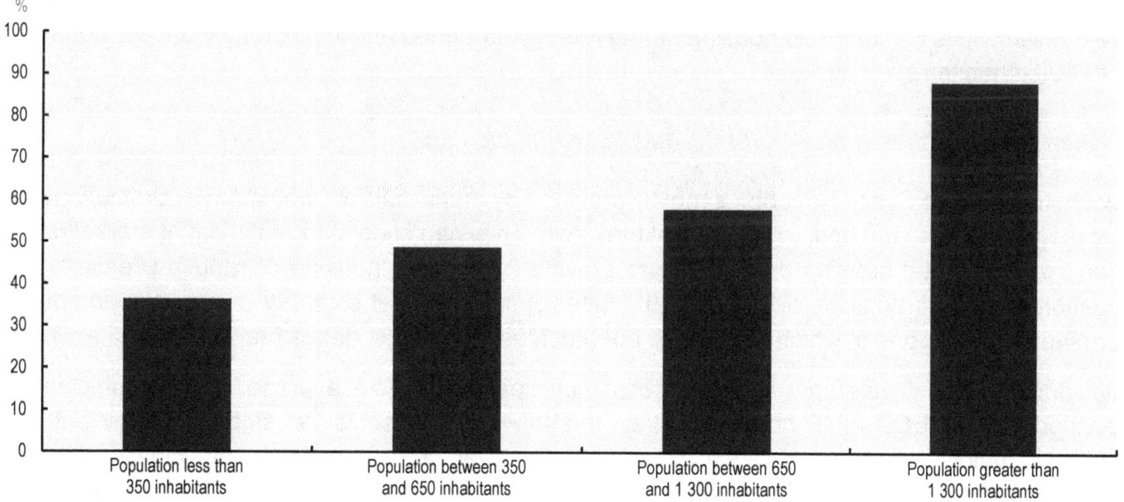

Source: OECD/MMR (2020[23]), *OECD-MMR Housing Survey of Municipalities in the Czech Republic*.

The shortage of social housing is visible in the long waiting lists of aspiring tenants applying for social housing. Among municipalities that allocate access to social housing through waiting lists, the median wait time is 24 months but, in 18% of municipalities, it can reach 60 months or longer (Figure 2.4).

Figure 2.4. Length of municipal waiting lists for social housing in municipalities in the Czech Republic

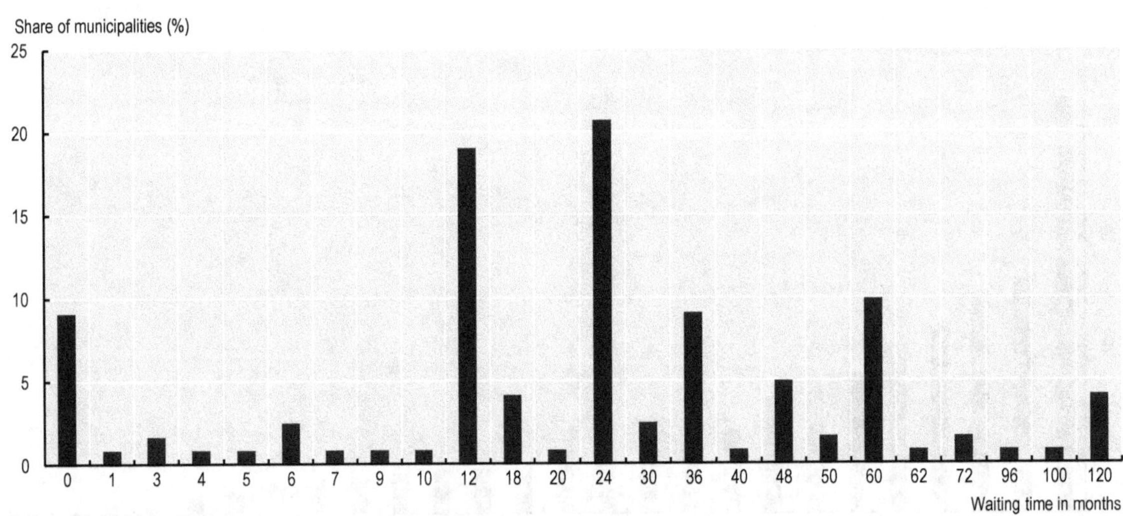

Note: Municipalities have different methods of allocating social housing (see following section). This figure refers to the 120 surveyed municipalities that provide access to social housing through waiting lists.
Source: OECD/MMR (2020[23]), *OECD-MMR Housing Survey of Municipalities in the Czech Republic*.

In light of such a shortage of social housing, it comes as no surprise that 35% of municipalities that responded to the OECD-MMR housing survey indicate that increasing the stock of social housing is a policy priority. However, only 15% of all municipalities built any housing between 2015 and 2019. Moreover, those municipalities that did build housing during this 5-year period only built on average 9.2 housing units per 10 000 inhabitants.[5]

Allocation of social housing varies across municipalities

Social housing in the Czech Republic is mostly provided by municipalities, which have complete autonomy in deciding how to use the housing stock that they own. They can choose to rent it out at market rates, just like any private rental housing provider, or to provide it as social housing at reduced rents to specific population groups. If municipalities choose the latter option, they set eligibility criteria autonomously and determine the conditions at which they rent it out (such as rent levels, deposit requirements, etc.).

Social housing rent levels vary widely across municipalities. In the average Czech municipality that responded to the OECD-MMR housing survey, monthly rents for social housing (i.e. municipal housing provided at below-market rates) are CZK 48/m². However, in a quarter of municipalities, rents are CZK 31/m² per month or less, while in another quarter of municipalities, rents are CZK 60/m² per month or higher. For comparison, the median monthly rents for municipal housing provided at market rate are approximately CZK 75/m².

Municipalities are not only free to choose how much social housing they provide and at what price; they can also determine who is eligible and how to allocate housing within the eligible population. In the absence of national binding guidelines, the allocation of social housing to households in need by individual municipalities is sometimes opaque and can prevent some households that need it the most from accessing social housing. Selection criteria for tenants in municipally owned housing can be unclear and may sometimes seem arbitrary or even potentially discriminatory. As illustrated in Table 2.2, which shows the various groups eligible for social housing, and Figure 2.5 on the selection criteria for allocating housing among eligible applicants, there is no common approach among municipalities. Selection criteria may include: time spent on a waiting list; social criteria such as age, family size, single-parent households, and people belonging to specific marginalised communities such as the Roma community (OECD, 2021[7]); special arrangements for the disabled and elderly; and the amount of a contribution tenants make to the municipality, without a clear and systematic record system of these contributions (OECD/MMR, 2020[23]).

Table 2.2. Eligibility for social housing in municipalities in the Czech Republic

Target group	Share of municipalities in which the target group is eligible for social housing (%)	Average number of dedicated units for the target group per 10 000 inhabitants
Elderly	82	48.4
Low-income households	74	17.1
Single parents	61	7.6
People with disabilities	50	5.5
Marginalised ethnic groups	41	3.3
Large families	46	1.7
Homeless	43	0.9
Other	60	21.5

Note: Results based on 198 municipalities indicate that they dedicate some social housing units to specific target groups. Beyond social housing dedicated to specific target groups, municipalities also provide social housing that is not dedicated to a specific group and is not included in this table.
Source: OECD/MMR (2020[23]), *OECD-MMR Housing Survey of Municipalities in the Czech Republic.*

Figure 2.5. Selection criteria for access to social housing in municipalities in the Czech Republic

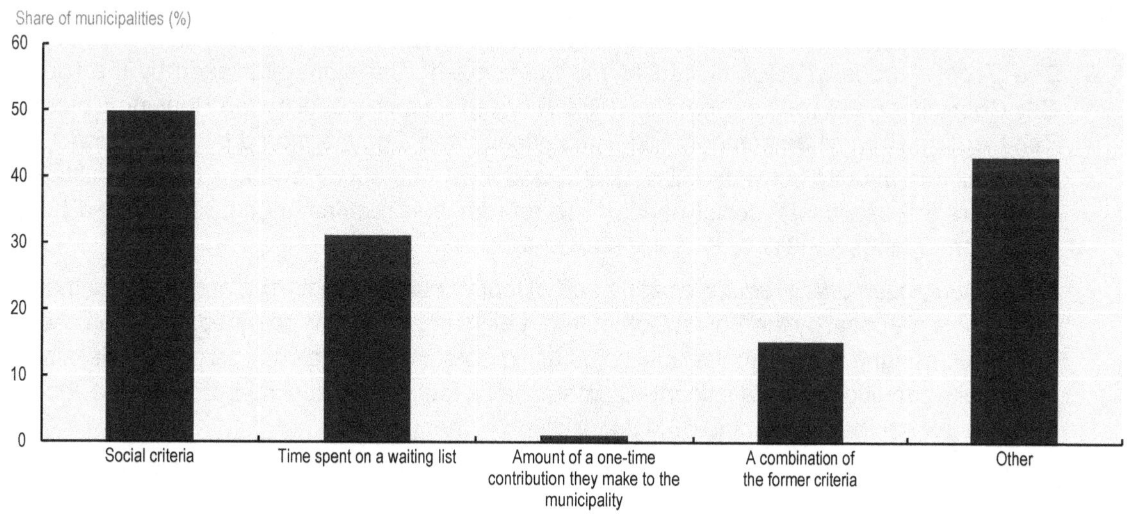

Source: OECD/MMR (2020[23]), *OECD-MMR Housing Survey of Municipalities in the Czech Republic.*

Beyond designating eligible groups for social housing, municipalities can introduce additional requirements that can further limit access to social housing for some population groups. In particular, such requirements may include deposit requirements and a ban on individuals who have a debt with the municipalities. Both requirements can prevent very low-income households from accessing social housing even though they are most urgently in need.

Most municipalities (64% of those who responded to the OECD-MMR housing survey) state that they do not require any deposit prior to granting access to social housing (Figure 2.6). However, when a deposit is required, in 22% of municipalities, it is CZK 6 000 or higher (i.e. about 1.3% of the average household net-adjusted annual disposable income) (OECD, 2020[24]). At such levels, the deposit can constitute a prohibitive factor that prevents low-income households from obtaining social housing even if they meet all other eligibility criteria, despite the possibility to use the housing allowance in order to pay a deposit. Likewise, about 90% of all surveyed municipalities do not provide housing to applicants that have a debt with the municipality. Often, these are former tenants of municipal housing who did not pay their rent. Just like deposit requirements, debt limitations are likely to affect the poorest households the hardest.

Box 2.5. A social and affordable housing plan interrupted in Olomouc

In Olomouc, 2019 saw the preparation of a Strategy of Affordable and Social Housing for the Statutory City of Olomouc 2020-23. Although the strategy should have entered the design stage in March 2020, its implementation has been postponed due to the ongoing COVID-19 crisis. The strategy is centred on five main goals:

- Prevent loss of housing.
- Create a permeable housing system allowing people to move from shelters to rental housing.
- Gradually transfer housing units from the regular municipal housing stock to the housing stock reserved for senior citizens and social housing.
- Maintain financial affordability and targeted allocation of flats to senior citizens and the disabled.
- Implement new multi-unit building projects on municipally owned land plots to be used as affordable housing for various target groups.

In Olomouc, the municipally owned housing stock can be divided into three types:

- *The "regular" housing stock owned by the municipality*: Decisions are taken by the Olomouc City Council or *Rada města Olomouce* (RMO) based on a proposal by the Housing Committee. The Housing Committee primarily takes into account the amount offered by the applicant to the city, which is usually between CZK 25 000 and CZK 100 000. However, the committee also considers the applicants' social needs. The rent for the "regular" municipally owned housing stock corresponds to 63%-73% of the market rent.
- *Special-purpose flats for senior citizens and disabled people*: Decisions are taken by the RMO based on a proposal by the Social Committee. Lease contracts are provided based on a waiting list, which assigns a score to the applicants using objective criteria such as age, social situation and health condition of the applicant. Olomouc has a total of 623 special-purpose flats, including 555 flats for senior citizens and 68 flats for disabled people.
- *Social flats*: Decisions on social flats are taken by the RMO based on a proposal by the Social and Housing Committees. Lease contracts are provided solely on the basis of the social needs of the applicants, usually to families in material need, to legally incompetent persons or persons leaving sheltered facilities. There are only 25 social housing units (flats) in Olomouc. The rent amount in both special-purpose flats and social flats is set by a decision of the Olomouc City Council and updated regularly. When setting the rent amount, the increase in market rent, development of old-age pensions and the quality of the housing stock are taken into account. As a result, social and special-purpose housing is rented out at an amount corresponding to 37%-50% of the market rent.

Recommendations

- Evaluate the balance between different types of municipally owned housing and, if possible, continue efforts to move housing units from the regular housing stock to the special-purpose and social housing stocks.
- Use municipally owned land to build affordable housing.
- Conclude joint development agreements with private developers.
- Make criteria for choosing successful applicants for the regular municipal housing stock more transparent.

Figure 2.6. Deposit requirements for social housing in municipalities in the Czech Republic

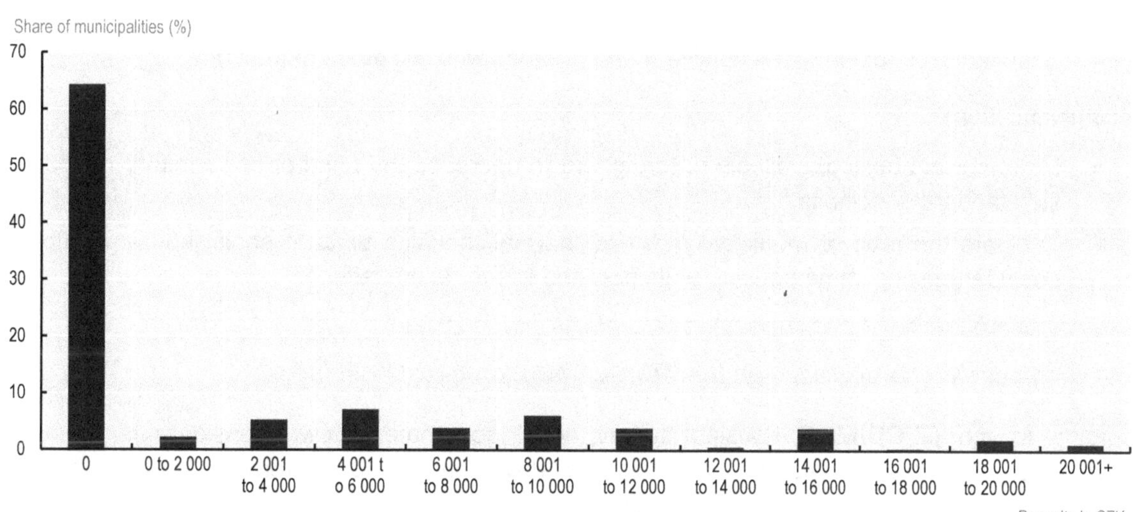

Source: OECD/MMR (2020[23]), *OECD-MMR Housing Survey of Municipalities in the Czech Republic*.

Deposit requirements and restrictions on debt prevent some eligible households from accessing social housing. By imposing financial preconditions on social housing, they are preventing some of the poorest households from accessing it, thereby excluding households that would need access to social housing most urgently. National guidelines on social housing could help co-ordinate social housing policies conducted by municipalities. The current lack of national guidelines has created an uneven landscape across the Czech Republic, in which social housing stocks, prices and eligibility requirements vary widely among municipalities. National guidelines could help provide a more equitable distribution of the available social housing stock and give priority to those who need it the most. Such guidelines should include a legal definition of social housing that enables all levels of government to regulate social housing more effectively.

Box 2.6. Social housing eligibility in Pilsen

The city of Pilsen owns approximately 2 901 flats, of which:

- 508 flats are reserved for seniors aged 65 or more and those with disability retirement. The rent in these flats is set at CZK 50 per m² per month.
- 107 flats are wheelchair-accessible and reserved for wheelchair users.

- 689 flats have reduced rents. These flats are offered to applicants based on their submitted application for a flat and the score awarded to their application.
- 45 social housing flats supported by social workers.

In Pilsen, all municipally owned flats are published online and residents can directly register for normal housing units. A social flat is a municipal flat that comes with the support of a social worker who carries out a comprehensive social survey for each applicant. Since May 2020, social flats are also published online for specific target groups (the elderly, disabled persons, young people and graduates, institutional care leavers, households needing the support of social workers, etc.).

The applicants are selected based on:

- Place of residence in Pilsen or employment in Pilsen.
- Income from employment – this does not apply to the elderly and disability pensioners.
- The current housing situation of the applicant.
- The health condition of the applicant and persons who will move to the flat.

Recommendations

- Make social housing available to foreigners to decrease the number of dormitory residents in substandard conditions.
- Evaluate the ratio of municipally owned "normal" housing units to social housing units and consider moving some housing units from the former to the latter.

Municipalities face obstacles in the development of social housing

According to the OECD-MMR housing survey, local governments own considerable amounts of undeveloped land that is suitable for housing development. On average, municipalities own 51 m²/inhabitant of undeveloped land that is suitable for housing construction, which is equivalent to approximately 9% of their built-up area. Publicly owned land is a strategic resource that can be mobilised in various ways for the provision of affordable housing, for example through joint developments with private investors that contain a large percentage of affordable housing units or through land leases that raise revenues for public housing construction on part of the land.

However, although Czech municipalities own significant amounts of developable land, there is a lack of investment in new social housing in general in the Czech Republic. In 2018, central government spending on social rental housing (encompassing both direct provisions of social rental housing and subsidies to non-governmental social rental housing providers) in the Czech Republic was only 0.01% of GDP, according to the OECD Affordable Housing Database. This is about 10 times less than the average of public spending by central governments of OECD countries for which data is available.

Several reasons could explain the low level of investment in new social housing. First, much of the municipally owned land suitable for development is located in small municipalities. According to the OECD-MMR housing survey, 71% of all municipally owned land belongs to municipalities that have fewer than 1 000 inhabitants (Figure 2.7). Such small municipalities might not have the administrative capacity that is needed to provide affordable housing on the land. Moreover, house prices in municipalities that own larger amounts of land per capita tend to be lower than house prices in municipalities that own less land, reducing the incentives to build more affordable housing.

Furthermore, the current legislative framework in the Czech Republic puts the responsibility of providing affordable housing and allocating social housing on municipalities, which may put smaller municipalities in the position of having to make politically risky decisions. Lux and Sunega (2017[25]) explain that "if decision-making is decentralized to a large number of agents that are financially and politically weak, these decentralised decision makers will have to take a strong risk in having to take responsibilities that are seen to be politically unpopular". Thus, municipalities may not have many incentives to expand their social housing stock as it may not gain them political favour (Lux and Sunega, 2017[25]).

Figure 2.7. Small municipalities own disproportionate amounts of land in the Czech Republic

Average amount of land suitable for development owned by municipalities, by population

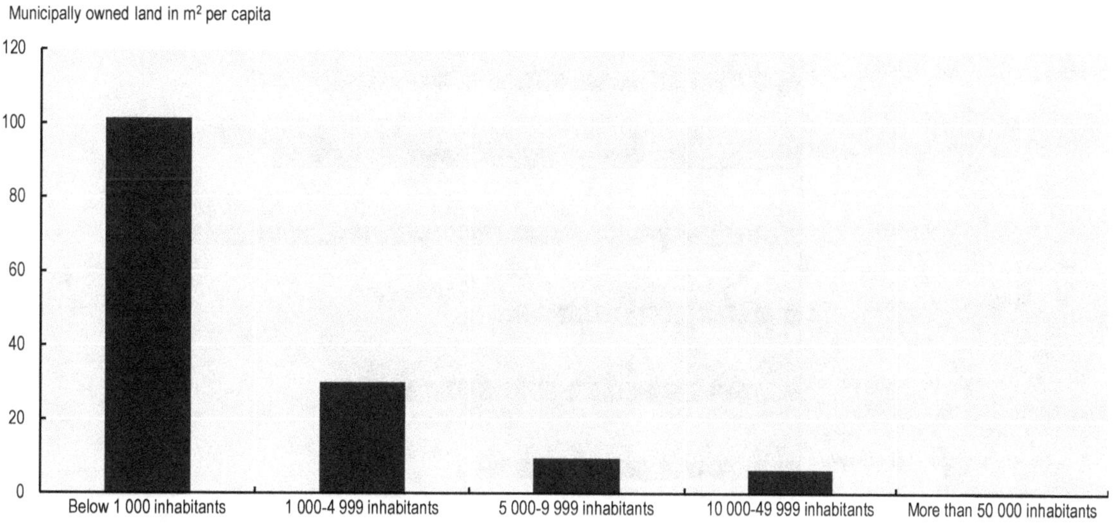

Source: OECD/MMR (2020[23]), *OECD-MMR Housing Survey of Municipalities in the Czech Republic.*

When municipalities do want to develop social housing, they are faced with a number of obstacles. The most important bottleneck to municipal housing development according to surveyed municipalities lies in the shortage of funds. On a scale from 0 (no importance) to 5 (high importance), municipalities list insufficient own financial resources and difficulties receiving state support as the two most important factors that prevent them from building housing (Figure 2.8). In particular, for smaller municipalities, an unwillingness to take on debt and insufficient administrative capacity are mentioned as equally important reasons. In contrast, access to credit is generally not seen as a major bottleneck, indicating that municipalities may be able to use this financing option but prefer not to do so.

More public investment in social housing is needed in cities

Given the general shortage of social housing, several local, national and EU investment schemes have already been put in place to help municipalities increase their social housing stock (EC, 2020[26]). For example:

- At the local level, the municipality of Ostrava, for example, has made social housing part of its long-term inclusiveness strategy. The project Social Housing in the City of Ostrava ran between 2016 and 2019 and was mostly funded by the European Social Fund (EUR 459 416 funded by the ESF out of a total investment amount of EUR 540 489). The municipality set aside municipal flats as they became available in its six most densely built and populated districts. After repairs, renovation and furnishing, 105 flats were made available to families who would otherwise live in substandard housing and now pay rent to the city that represents about half the cost of private rent (EC, 2018[27]).

Figure 2.8. Bottlenecks for municipal housing construction in municipalities in the Czech Republic

Average ranking by municipalities from 0 (no importance) – 5 (very high importance)

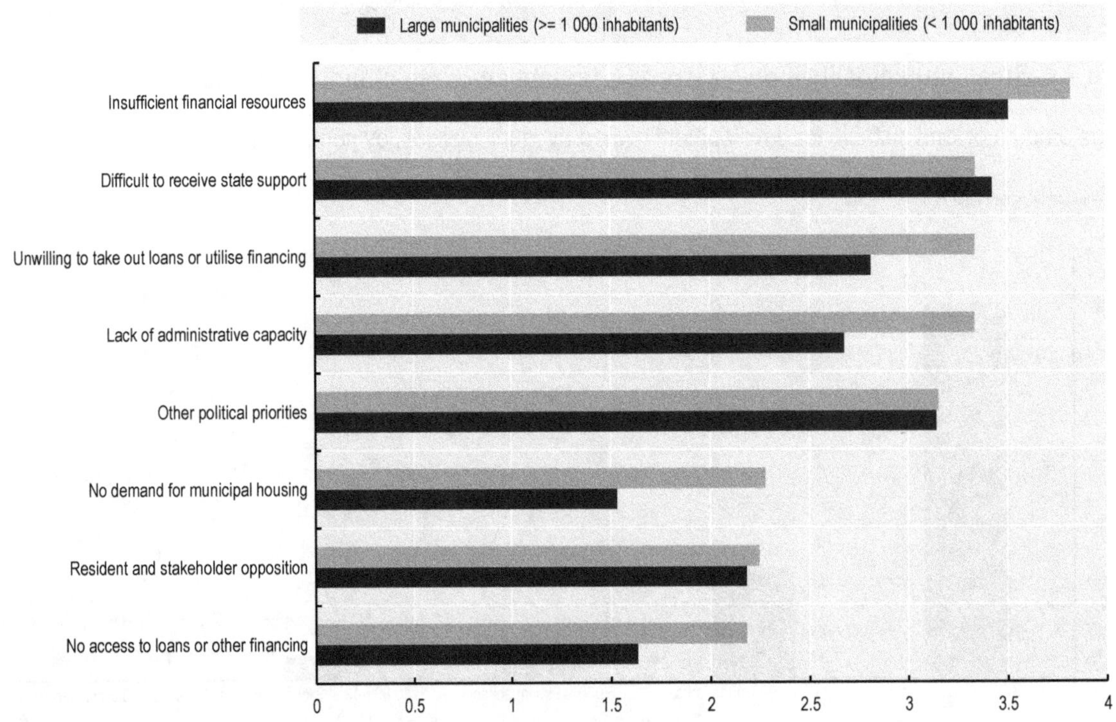

Source: OECD/MMR (2020[23]), *OECD-MMR Housing Survey of Municipalities in the Czech Republic.*

- At the national level, support is provided by the MMR and the SISF. The MMR mainly provides grants to municipalities for the creation or renovation of the housing stock intended for specific population groups, such as low-income households, elderly people, people with disabilities, etc. The Housing Support programme, for example, promotes the construction or acquisition of social housing rental flats for people with special needs such as age, health or social circumstances (MMR, 2018[5]). The SISF also supports the construction of social housing. Cities can benefit from this loan programme to buy social flats or houses, or combine the acquisition of social and affordable flats in one building in so-called "mixed houses" (Office of the Government, 2019[28]). However, these schemes are still not enough to make a difference, both due to the size of investments and their modalities.

Managing publicly owned land more strategically and using it to provide affordable housing where possible is key to foster more construction of social housing. In places where prices are already high, municipalities should aim at using this land for the provision of affordable housing, for example by concluding joint development agreements with private developers, taking into consideration the small number of not-for-profit housing providers. Developers can be incentivised to build affordable housing through loans, grants and subsidies. Inclusionary zoning, in which a specific minimum percentage of new housing units must be reserved by developers to be rented at below-market price, could also increase affordable housing provision while also expanding the private rental market. Innovative schemes such as issuing social housing bonds or encouraging real estate investment trust (REIT) schemes focusing on investing in social housing can be leveraged in these cases. Where prices are currently low or where publicly owned land cannot be developed for other reasons, municipalities should treat publicly owned land as a strategic resource that can help them provide affordable housing in the future. Where possible, infrastructure investments and other urban planning decisions should help enable the future use of municipal land for affordable housing development. Likewise, decisions to sell public land should be made only after taking a long-term perspective on the potential value of the land for the municipality.

Furthermore, reducing the shortage of social housing will require greater public investment by the national and local governments. Currently, municipal housing construction is low even though it is a political objective for many municipalities to increase social housing provision. As a consequence, long waiting lists for social housing persist and a significant number of people have little choice but to live in dormitories and other forms of substandard accommodation. Additional financial support from the national government for social housing development is indispensable to provide affordable housing to every person in need of it. Moreover, state support to municipalities should be made available ahead of construction to avoid that short-term financing constraints deter municipalities from undertaking social housing development.

Better utilising the existing social housing stock and expanding it will require co-ordinated action between national and local levels of government. Moreover, they should ensure co-ordination across municipalities within functional urban areas (FUAs) to take into account the fact that the need for and availability of social housing are uneven across municipalities.

The private rental sector could be further strengthened to provide more affordable options, especially to low- and middle-income households in cities

Sufficient stock of affordable rental housing is a key component of an affordable housing market. Rental housing is the only solution for low-income households as well as the "squeezed" middle class that are not eligible for social housing but are also unable to afford mortgages to purchase their own home. Moreover, rental housing is usually available at much shorter notice than owner-occupied housing and social housing. The private rental market is currently limited and does not provide enough affordable housing to Czech households. Only 17.5% of Czech households rented their property from the private market in 2018. Both demand- and supply-side issues are at the root of the relatively small private rental sector. On the supply side, investors are often not interested in expanding this sector, partly because of the high cost of construction. Many developers have not yet recovered from the 2009 financial crisis and are now waiting until construction costs decrease before continuing projects. Furthermore, supply is restricted by several entry barriers which hinder access to rental housing for many low-income and middle-class households. For example, to be able to rent a house or a flat, aspiring tenants need to pay a deposit and several months of rent in advance, which many low-income households cannot afford. Several population groups are also reported to face specific barriers to access rental housing (e.g. the Roma community, people with mental health issues, etc.). On the demand side, there is a strong individual preference towards ownership, even among younger people who adhere to the strong social norms favouring homeownership, as seen in Chapter 1 (Lux et al., 2017[29]). Additionally, the quality of the private rental stock may be poor. Lux and Sunega have found that private rental housing is associated with "high costs, a small number of rooms, a low technical standard (problems with humidity, insufficient light or external noise), and a location in the less developed Czech regions" (2010[30]). As a result, private rental housing is more often seen as transitional housing than as a valid alternative to homeownership.

In order to encourage the development of the private rental sector, the State Investment Promotion Fund (SIPF) has implemented the Rental Housing Development Programme, consisting of loans to support the construction or regeneration of rental housing for specific population groups that may have difficulties entering the housing market (e.g. seniors, youth, disabled persons, etc.). Municipalities, businesses and individuals may apply for these loans. Uptake has been limited, with two contracts granted in 2019 and only one in 2020.

Although the stock of rental housing in the Czech Republic is low by international standards, municipalities give the provision of rental housing a very low priority. Only 11% of all surveyed municipalities indicated that increasing the stock of rental housing is a policy priority, even though 46% of all municipalities were in favour of increasing the supply of privately built housing. Given the importance of rental housing for low-income households and the low stock of rental housing in the Czech Republic, public policies at all levels of government should encourage the construction and provision of rental housing. National incentives to increase the stock of rental housing must be better structured to allow municipalities to leverage them.

Furthermore, the Czech Republic could support the rental housing market further by implementing other policies to increase the supply and demand for private rental housing. Measures to support specifically the rental market exist in several countries across the OECD. Such measures include tax relief measures for renters, rent guarantees and deposits, and minimum quality regulations for rental dwellings. Eleven countries among those surveyed by the OECD (Australia, Belgium, Costa Rica, Germany, Japan, Luxembourg, Mexico, Norway, Portugal, Sweden and the United Kingdom) have reported that they offer rent guarantees and deposits. These can be structured to reduce risks of rent loss for landlords or to support tenants who cannot afford to pay the initial deposits necessitated by rentals. Given the inability of many Czech would-be tenants to pay these kinds of deposits, such a policy could benefit the Czech rental market and enable households to move from dormitories to the private rental market. Finally, most countries in the OECD have a legal requirement in place to ensure a minimum level of quality of dwellings available for rent (OECD, 2019[4]). Coupled with a robust scheme to fund and facilitate the renovation of private rental properties, minimum quality requirements for rental dwellings could ensure a better quality of life for tenants. Care should however be given to avoid an unintended shrinking of the rental market due to excessive quality requirements. Other innovative models attempting to use the private rental market for social purposes, such as social rental agencies, could be considered.

However, strengthening of the rental sector could further increase the incidence of short-term rentals through peer-to-peer accommodation rental Internet platforms in touristic cities such as Prague, where the share of short-term rentals has already been growing rapidly to as much as one-quarter of flats rented out for tourist short-term rentals in Prague's Old Town, as discussed in Chapter 1. As the rise in these short-term rentals has led to a decline in available and affordable rental flats for regular tenants, Czech authorities need to implement regulation to limit the negative effects of this phenomenon on affordable housing. Such regulation has been implemented in several other OECD countries, both by national and local governments. In Amsterdam, for example, owners may only offer their dwellings for a limited number of days per year (60) for short-term rental purposes and dwellings offered for short-term rental must be registered with the municipality. Norway introduced a ban on short-term rental for more than 90 days a year. In Mexico, the Income Tax and Value Added Tax Laws establish that the host incomes for short-term/holiday rentals are subject to tax payment. In the United States, New Orleans has implemented a prohibition of short-term rentals in the French Quarter and taxation of bookings executed through Airbnb. Los Angeles has similar restrictions (Cournède, Ziemann and De Pace, 2020[31]).

Housing co-operatives could be retooled and non-governmental actors activated to strengthen housing affordability objectives

Housing co-operatives provide accommodation possibilities to their members. They became popular in the post-war Czech Republic because most construction costs could be financed by state loans and more efficient housing structures (i.e. multi-unit buildings, prefabricated buildings) could be constructed than by any one household alone. Today, residents are legally allowed to sell the right to live in housing co-operatives. This is due to provisions enacted to curb grey market trading of housing shares.

European Union (EU) state aid rules in relation to the support of housing outside of social housing are rather strict, complicating the ways the national government can support non-governmental actors in the provision of affordable housing. The EU Urban Agenda Housing Partnership's guidance paper on EU regulation and public support for housing stipulates that "non-financial measures are also available to authorities to support investments in affordable, adequate and social housing without being labelled as state aid under EU rules. E.g.: Support the creation and capacity of institutions and organisations that will contribute to social and affordable housing such as not-for-profit investors, Community Land Trusts, housing cooperatives and public companies" (EU Urban Agenda Housing Partnership, 2017[32]). Despite the low amount of not-for-profit housing providers currently, there is untapped potential for new models of housing provision in the Czech Republic. Not-for-profit investors in housing can include non-profit organisations but could also be reached through public-private partnerships. Other forms of organisations that could be strengthened include community land trusts, in which a non-profit corporation holds land on behalf of the community. Such non-financial measures like supporting non-profits as housing providers could be leveraged to support further the co-operative housing sector.

Box 2.7. Characteristics of Czech housing co-operatives

- Members are tenants and not owners of the flats. Housing units remain the property of the housing co-operative.
- Most of the housing co-operatives operate as non-profit organisations and do not create profit.
- Housing co-operatives are managed professionally or voluntarily (9 700 housing co-operatives were established with the privatisation procedure, with 150 000 housing units managed by volunteers. The remaining 280 000 units are managed by professionals).
- Members of the housing unit pay a share for the management of the housing co-operative.
- The monthly rent paid by members of the housing co-operative is determined according to the used floor area.
- The rent paid for the flat covers the cost of a mortgage, insurance premiums, maintenance of the building and fee for managing the housing company (in 2011, the monthly fee amounted to EUR 6-8 per housing unit).

Source: Lipej, B. and G. Turel (2018[33]), "Housing cooperatives as an opportunity for solving the housing issue", http://dx.doi.org/10.26262/RELAND.V1I0.6478.

Urban households that cannot access the private rental market currently rely on substandard housing and need targeted support

Some low-income households cannot access private rental housing due to high rents and deposit requirements. Moreover, some population groups may be exposed to risks of discriminatory practices if some landlords are reluctant to rent flats to them even if the latter have the necessary financial means. This could be particularly the case for homeless people, ethnic minorities, immigrants, people with mental illnesses, families with children, households with at least one person in long-term unemployment, households with low-skilled workers, single mothers and single-person pensioner households. Accessing municipal social housing also often turns out to be difficult, due to limited provision of social housing and long waiting lists as discussed earlier in this chapter. Czech households that cannot access either social housing or the private rental sector may be eligible for crisis housing or rely on dormitories. Crisis housing is usually provided by not-for-profit organisations through subsidies from the Ministry of Labour and Social Affairs, for which there is no specific legislation. Temporary crisis housing owned by not-for-profit organisations is operated as social services for people in acute housing need, such as the homeless, victims of domestic violence, refugees or ethnic minorities (Lux and Sunega, 2017[25]). However, social housing provision by non-governmental organisations remains very rare. According to the OECD-MMR housing survey, it exists only in 5% of all surveyed municipalities and the number of housing units provided tends to be low, at 3.6 housing units per 10 000 inhabitants. Furthermore, approximately half of these units were built within the past five years, indicating that this is a relatively recent approach that has the potential to grow in the future.

Box 2.8. Homelessness in Olomouc

In Olomouc, the number of homeless people out of the total population is slightly below the national average. However, the average age of homeless people and duration of homelessness are significantly above the Czech average. The city has a well-established ecosystem of homelessness prevention and management, with shelters for both men and women with children, dormitories and other services. The municipality's main challenges regarding homelessness include complaints from city residents about residents of shelters and dormitories, a shortage of shelters for families with children (even though there are shelters for mothers with children, as noted above), repeated stays in shelters or dormitories due to the inaccessibility of regular housing for people who have experienced homelessness and the prevalence of mental illness and addiction among residents in shelters and dormitories.

Recommendations

- Increase access to social housing for dormitory residents to curb repeated stays in dormitories and provide stable housing.
- Implement short-term solutions, including creating family shelters, while working to facilitate access to private rental housing.

As the number of crisis housing units is low, many households have no choice but to turn to alternative housing with substandard conditions, such as dormitories. As discussed in Chapter 1, these facilities frequently provide housing to migrant workers and marginalised population groups, such as the Roma. Residents in dormitories do not have standard rental contracts or a local residence permit. Rents can be extremely expensive for low-quality accommodation including shared facilities and frequent overcrowding (ECSR, 2020[34]). Although tenants in rental housing are typically granted some statutory protections, people living in dormitories are not usually granted these (ECSR, 2020[34]), although tenants of those dormitories approved by the regional hygiene board are eligible for housing benefits. Not only do residents of these dormitories lack security of tenure but there is a heightened risk of eviction for discriminated-against groups and Roma citizens in particular.

Box 2.9. Dormitories in Pilsen

In Pilsen, there are a number of privately-run dormitories but the municipality also owns one. As of 30 September 2018, there was a total of 4 838 beds in approved dormitories (1 450 beds when excluding dormitories for students and employees). The dormitory operated by the municipality of Pilsen offers accommodation for people who are without shelter. The aim is to provide immediately available housing to people who currently find themselves on the street and can benefit from the support of social workers until they can find adequate long-term housing.

In 2014, through the Social Services Department of Pilsen City Council, the municipality of Pilsen commissioned an analysis entitled "Latent Homelessness" aimed at mapping the dormitories in Pilsen and the composition of their residents. The largest group in dormitories consisted of foreigners (40.5% of respondents). The most common reason for coming to Pilsen was to look for a job (75.5% of respondents). Alarmingly, 22.1% of respondents had never had permanent housing. Furthermore, observations conducted in dormitories showed deprived environments, with residents feeling frustrated and angry because of the barriers they face in accessing housing, including discrimination due to ethnicity, debt, the composition of their family and the high levels of required deposits by landlords.

Recommendations

- Increase access to social housing to decrease the number of the "chronically" homeless population, as it is clear that the barriers to accessing permanent housing result in high rates of dormitory residents who have never had access to permanent housing or repeatedly stay in dormitories.
- Implement measures to increase access to the private rental market.
- Make social housing available to foreigners.

National regulations of dormitories should therefore be strengthened to protect residents and improve their living conditions. National regulations of dormitories should include provisions on minimum quality requirements (e.g. number of residents per room, number of bathrooms, etc.) and provide increased statutory protection for residents. While national and local governments should ultimately aim at eliminating the need for dormitories, short-term regulations have to strike a balance between increasing the protection of residents and avoiding the closure of dormitories. As dormitories often constitute a last-resort option for residents, regulations that would lead to their closure would leave residents worse off unless viable alternative forms of accommodation exist.

Indirect instruments could better support housing affordability objectives in cities

Responsiveness of housing supply to housing demand is one of the main factors affecting housing prices. In addition to policies directly aiming to increase the supply of affordable housing, other policy instruments affect the framework conditions for affordable housing supply indirectly. In the Czech Republic, several policy areas do not currently create favourable conditions for the development of affordable housing. For example, spatial and land use planning instruments do not sufficiently advance housing affordability goals and complex building regulations slow down the construction process, putting a large burden on developers and thus limiting housing supply. There is a lack of co-ordination between housing and transport policies and on housing development between municipalities, creating inefficiencies and potentially leading to urban sprawl. Finally, the subnational government fiscal framework is not conducive to providing municipalities with the resources to increase the supply of affordable housing. There is potential in each of these domains to streamline processes and align incentives.

Spatial and land use planning systems are not directly aligned with housing affordability objectives

When aligned with housing affordability objectives, land use and spatial planning can be used to steer new developments and urban growth in a sustainable manner while supporting housing affordability. Planning can contribute to affordable housing in several ways. First, planning can enable a sufficient supply of housing by zoning land appropriately, while taking care to prevent sprawl. Ensuring that housing supply matches demand can prevent house prices from rising and thus promote housing affordability. Second, specific planning instruments can be used to target housing affordability. These include land value capture instruments such as inclusionary zoning, which requires that a given share of new housing has to be affordable to low- and moderate-income households. While this approach works only where land prices are high, it can target specific population groups or low-income households broadly and encourage the development of affordable housing. Moreover, planning can generally influence the type of housing that is built (e.g. multi- vs. single-family housing). In some countries, zoning regulations or developer obligations can include requirements on unit sizes. This can ensure that housing development is in line with the requirements of the population while supporting the development of compact cities.

In several OECD countries, local zoning and land use planning policies often hamper housing construction and limit housing supply, contributing significantly to high housing costs. In the Czech Republic, however, there is little indication of that happening, since municipalities have zoned large areas of undeveloped land for residential development. In municipalities covered by the OECD-MMR housing survey, an average of 79 m²/inhabitant of greenfield land is zoned for development in local master plans. This corresponds to approximately 15% of the current built-up area of the municipalities covered by the survey. As there is little construction activity on land that is zoned for development, it is likely that the large majority of municipal zoning plans does not create bottlenecks for housing construction.

Yet, the Czech planning system does not seem to contribute to steering housing development in areas with high prices either. According to the OECD-MMR housing survey, there is no relationship between the amount of greenfield land per inhabitant within a municipality that is zoned for development and the level of house prices (Figure 2.9). On average, municipalities with very low price levels have zoned the same amount of land for development as municipalities with very high price levels, which suggests that the planning system does not contribute to reversing the pattern of untargeted housing development described in Chapter 1.

Figure 2.9. No correlation between price levels and amount of greenfield land zoned for development

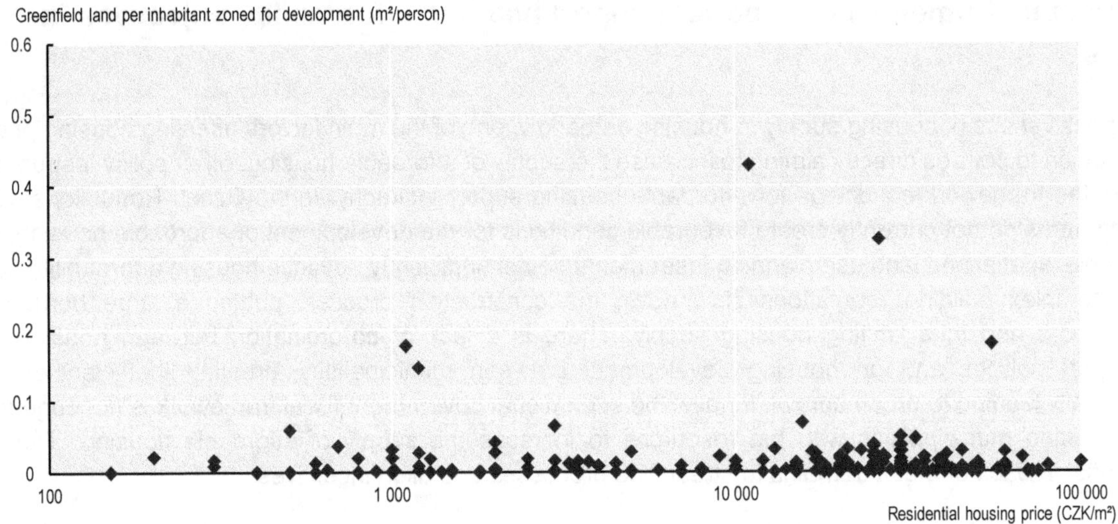

Source: OECD/MMR (2020[23]), *OECD-MMR Housing Survey of Municipalities in the Czech Republic.*

This lack of planning direction is also apparent when considering that the average amount of undeveloped land suitable for development is significant, at 304 m²/inhabitant across municipalities. Figure 2.10 shows how there are significant amounts of unutilised land even in municipalities where housing is expensive, albeit to a lesser degree than in municipalities where housing is cheap. Land use planning systems together with zoning regulations are not utilising the full potential of undeveloped land, even in municipalities where demand for housing is high.

Box 2.10. Land use planning in Pilsen

The Pilsen Land Use Plan has been in effect since 1 October 2016. It defines the main objectives that underpin the city's urban development, in particular the different types of use for individual areas which:

- "create the preconditions for sustained development of the City of Pilsen as a strong economic, administrative, cultural and social centre of the Pilsen Region;
- are in compliance with the sustainable development principles, i.e. harmonisation of economic growth, social cohesion and high quality of the environment, and thus create preconditions for healthy growth of the City of Pilsen;
- provide for a great variety of use, including adequate spatial regulation and specifying public space areas, and thus creates territorial conditions for development of the City of Pilsen as a pleasant place to live, work and spend leisure time;
- create preconditions for further development of the main urban functions by outlining areas suitable for reconstruction/transformation and buildable areas, with the requirement to preserve the environmental stability of the territory and to create conditions for adequate transport and technical infrastructure to be developed there."

The Land Use Plan also defines the basic principles for land use planning, as it:

- Prefers an intensive use of the built-up area by reasonable densification of development in terms of compliance with the land use regulations specifying individual areas with a different type of use to acquisition of agricultural land and natural sites.
- Consistently complies with the compact city principles.
- Outlines areas suitable for reconstruction/transformation and proposes a new method for their use.
- Limits development on high-quality agricultural land with the aim of ensuring maximum protection of agricultural land subject to the first and second levels of protection.
- Proposes buildable areas that should be further developed, preferably in connection with the built-up area.
- Proposes buildable areas that should be further developed in a manner preventing demanding traffic conditions and preferring locations with existing or predicted high-quality municipal public transportation service.
- Defines the individual land use areas predominantly as polyfunctional. It specifies their main use (if defined) and a great variety of acceptable types of use and at the same time those that are forbidden.
- Rules out the development of heavy industry and other industries and activities which negatively impact the environment and lead to high transport requirements.
- Confirms and further strengthens the role of floodplain zones of individual rivers and confirms that such areas must not be developed.

Based on the latest population and housing census (PHC), there were 79 964 housing units in 2011 in Pilsen, of which approximately 80% were in multi-unit buildings. Since 2012, 3 620 new housing units have been built, bringing the total housing stock to 83 584 housing units at the end of 2020. As mentioned before, Pilsen is one of the most expensive cities in the Czech Republic and many households have encountered difficulties accessing the housing market. However, as is the case in many other municipalities surveyed by the OECD-MMR housing survey, there is no indication in Pilsen of local zoning and land use planning policies hampering construction and limiting housing supply.

Pilsen indicates that on greenfield land zoned for development, there could be between 12 000 and 17 000 new units built while, on brownfield land, there could be another 6 500 to 9 000 housing units built. Taking the lowest estimate of this potential for more units, this is twice as much as the overall number of units built between 1999 and 2020. Land use planning systems together with zoning regulation in Pilsen are therefore not utilising the full potential of undeveloped land.

Recommendations

In order to increase housing supply for all in desired locations, the city of Pilsen could:

- Further leverage local land use planning and zoning instruments to encourage private-sector construction of affordable housing in desired locations.
- Broaden the use of developer obligations within local land use planning policies such as inclusionary zoning (i.e. the requirement on developers to provide a share of housing units in new developments as affordable rental units).

Figure 2.10. Amount of undeveloped land suitable for development by housing price bracket

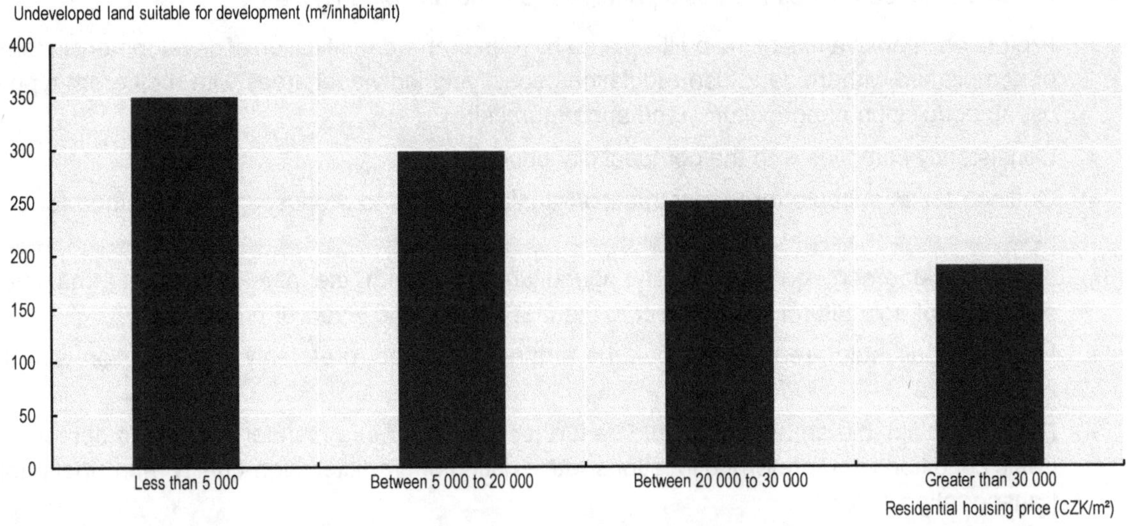

Source: OECD/MMR (2020[23]), *OECD-MMR Housing Survey of Municipalities in the Czech Republic.*

In the Czech Republic, limited use is being made of spatial and land use planning tools to increase housing affordability. Municipalities are responsible for local land use planning and development. Even though the hierarchy of plans has higher-order national plans demanding conformity from lower-order local ones, the central government has difficulty influencing planning policies at the municipal level. At the municipal level, developers can have an outsized impact on land use planning. As has been elaborated in previous OECD work (2017[35]), gaps between plans and planning processes, greenfield development and the ensuing urban sprawl, and a lack of political awareness and willingness to use planning tools currently undermine housing affordability objectives.

Generally, planning lacks both vertical and horizontal co-ordination. This can be observed by the divide between regional policy and spatial planning, and in the conflicts between sectoral and spatial plans. Czech spatial management is determined by both regional policy and spatial planning (OECD, 2017[35]). Despite attempts at co-ordination and some overlapping, there are missing links between the two. Because regional policy (which tends to focus on economic development) and strategic planning are separated from territorial planning, planning is rendered less effective and separated from the state's financial plans. As a result, municipalities may make statutory plans without clearly anchoring them in public budgets, leading to a mismatch between resources and ambitions (OECD, 2017[35]). Furthermore, sectoral divisions have led to a fragmented approach to sustainable land management in the Czech Republic (Petřík, Fanta and Petrtýl, 2015[36]). The lack of integration between sectoral and spatial plans can lead to conflicts between land uses. Such conflicts can emerge, for example, between the preservation of historical monuments or natural assets and projects for transportation infrastructure. Conflicts also occur between the desire to protect good agricultural land and the desire for new residential and other forms of development (OECD, 2017[35]). In some cities, such as Pilsen, the land use plan limits development on high-quality agricultural land, while implementing compact city principles.

Despite the need for more housing construction, care must be taken to prevent urban sprawl by planning for more compact cities. In commuting zones of Czech cities, new residential developments have mushroomed. This type of urban sprawl leads to higher infrastructure and service costs, while also fragmenting land. Current land use regulation has enabled much of recent developments to take place on previously arable land, with approximately 9 100 hectares (ha) of agricultural land being lost per year (Janků et al., 2016[37]). Municipalities tend to be very positive about population growth as tax revenues are largely based on the number of inhabitants. Moreover, selling the hitherto agricultural land as developable land multiplies the yield for (local) landowners. However, legal protection of the most valuable agricultural land is in force (OECD, 2017[35]). Janků et al. (2016[37]) cite several potential causes for the ongoing development of urban sprawl in the Czech Republic, including increasing demand for a "greener, more attractive, and family-friendly environment" with better quality housing and more living space per capita to be found in peri-urban areas. To reverse this trend of urban sprawl, cities need to do more to create attractive mid- to high-density neighbourhoods. This will especially have to be taken into consideration in the wake of the ongoing COVID-19 crisis. Increasing demand for green space and less dense living environments may very well be a lasting legacy of the crisis. This will have to be closely monitored and the environmental benefits of density should not be undermined.

In addition to residential developments, commercial and industrial developments often occur on greenspace. The transport infrastructure needed to sustain commercial and industrial activity leads to their development close to major roads on lands that often have good soil. Warehouses, logistics and shopping centres, manufacturing and business parks are thus poised to take up high-grade soil. Complicating the issue of new development are the many old industrial, or brownfield, sites in the Czech Republic. These can be industrial, agricultural or military in nature. Brownfield sites account for a considerable share of most Czech cities' territory. Brownfield regeneration provides cities with a valuable opportunity to prevent the loss of green spaces, enhance urban spaces and create a new housing supply. Furthermore, brownfield sites are usually well connected within the urban boundaries, offering a competitive alternative to greenfield investment (OECD, 2018[38]). Even though these sites represent potential development sites and their redevelopment should be encouraged, they can be very difficult to revitalise. Industrial brownfields can have fragmented ownership and/or leasing rights, agricultural brownfields are often in remote locations and military lands often contain contaminated soil (OECD, 2017[35]). The remediation required by brownfield sites poses an obstacle to their use as municipalities may lack the funds required for their rehabilitation. In order to make use of brownfield sites while encouraging the development of affordable housing, programmes giving tax breaks or subsidies to developers for land remediation in return for the provision of affordable housing could be considered.

In order to improve housing affordability in urban areas where housing demand is high and prevent sprawl and vacant housing in areas where demand for housing is low, housing development needs to target urban areas where prices are high. However, as examined in Chapter 1, housing development in the Czech Republic has been unrelated to price levels. According to the OECD-MMR housing survey, when housing construction does happen, it does not seem to focus on high-priced areas, with no indication that municipalities with higher price levels have experienced increased construction activity. In other words, growth in demand (reflected in higher prices) has not been met by an increase in supply. In contrast, many municipalities with low price levels experienced considerable housing development. In these municipalities, there is a risk that this housing development creates undesired side-effects such as high vacancy rates and urban sprawl. To prevent this, national and regional planning frameworks need to provide clearer guidance to local planning policies on where housing development should occur or not. Where necessary, these guidelines should also have a binding force on local governments. In turn, municipalities should actively strive to adapt their planning policies more effectively to local housing markets. Where prices are high, planning policies should encourage high-density housing development. Where prices are low, local zoning should be restrictive to prevent overdevelopment and its associated negative fiscal and environmental consequences.

The use of developer obligations within local land use planning policies could be broadened. In particular, many OECD countries have used inclusionary zoning (i.e. the requirement on developers to provide a share of housing units in new developments as affordable rental units) successfully to improve housing affordability in the most expensive cities. For example, most major cities in Germany use inclusionary zoning and related instruments extensively. In 2020, the city of Frankfurt passed a new regulation that not only requires the provision of 30% affordable rental units in greenfield developments but also the provision of 10% affordable owner-occupied units, 15% co-operative units and 15% free-market rental units. Such regulation is especially suitable for urban areas where prices are very high. It needs to be used more carefully in contexts where prices are less high, as it may stifle housing supply and increase prices if it reduces incentives for developers to build housing.

Complex building regulations and skills shortages in the construction sector slow down construction and increase construction costs. The complexity and time-intensive nature of construction in the Czech Republic is an obstacle to affordable housing. The Building Act (Act No. 183/2006 Coll. on Spatial Planning and Building Regulations) is the main legal regulation in construction in the Czech Republic. It deals with the duties and responsibilities of the participants in the construction process, territorial planning, construction permits or other necessary rules and actions needed for the realisation of construction works. As discussed in Chapter 1, the current administrative procedures to obtain building permits are a major hurdle to the increase in housing supply, with the Czech Republic ranking 157 out of 190 countries in the World Bank Group's *Doing Business 2020* report in the area of dealing with construction permits (World Bank Group, 2020[39]).

In order to speed up and streamline the permitting process, the Building Act and related laws are set to be reformed. The new law is expected to take effect in 2023. The renewed building permit process aims to give citizens the opportunity to obtain a building permit within one year of submitting an application, including a possible appeal against a decision and judicial review. The MMR is aiming to integrate currently separate processes, including the issuance of binding opinions, zoning decisions and building permits, into a single procedure. While this reform is expected to accelerate and greatly streamline the procedures for the average citizen and the larger investor, the planned change will be demanding on the management and internal organisation of work within building authorities. A key condition for the successful setup and operation of the new system is the overall digitisation of administrative proceedings and documents for issuing decisions (MMR, n.d.[40]). The impact of this reform should be monitored to make sure the procedures are accelerated and streamlined, both for individual citizens and for large developers.

Minimum parking requirements should be abolished to reduce construction costs and encourage housing construction within urban centres. Such requirements drive construction costs up especially in densely populated city centres, where the cost of providing the parking space often exceeds the price of the car that uses it. Moreover, they create high social costs as they take up valuable public space and encourage car use over public transport (Shoup, 2017[41]).

Better aligning housing policy with transport, energy and other policies could improve housing affordability in Czech cities

As discussed in Chapter 1, the ability to rent or buy housing is only one measure of its affordability. Households must also be able to afford to live in accommodation, meaning they must be able to shoulder the maintenance and utility costs that come with their accommodation. Two specific areas that may contribute to overburdening a household's finances outside of rent or mortgage are transport and energy. Cheaper housing far away from a city centre may lead to a long commute with high fuel costs, increasing the overall cost of housing and decreasing well-being. Low-income households may be able to save on rent by living in older, non-refurbished buildings with less efficient appliances but pay a significantly higher energy bill as a result (Ugarte et al., 2016[42]). Transport and energy must thus be considered in tandem with housing affordability policies to adopt an integrated and holistic approach to housing affordability.

The integration of housing and transport is particularly relevant, as they have an outsized impact on both the quality and cost of living for urban residents and on the wider economic and environmental outcomes (Heeckt and Huerta, n.d.[43]). Seemingly more affordable housing might not only come with higher transport costs but can also reduce access to public services, public space and economic opportunities. Furthermore, if housing is more affordable on the outskirts of cities, these cities may not be able to retain the population density needed to sustain local businesses and infrastructures. The current national transport framework in place in the Czech Republic is a comprehensive document including both objectives and strategic priorities and a section on monitoring (Czech Ministry of Transport, 2013[44]). However, both this document and the national housing framework lack co-ordination and linkages.

Better integrating the housing sector with transport and favouring transit-oriented development would not only improve housing affordability but also encourage sustainable urban development. Around the world, demand for transport is set to increase so sharply that even if current and announced mitigation policies are implemented, worldwide transport CO_2 emissions are projected to grow by 60% by 2050 (ITF, 2019[45]). Although emissions from urban passenger transport are projected to fall by 19% worldwide, the focus on sustainable urban transport enabling this decline should not be let out of sight: indeed, 14.5% of greenhouse gas emissions in the Czech Republic were due to the transport sector in 2017 (OECD, n.d.[46]). Though this is well below the OECD average of 23.57%, the Czech Republic should consider it a priority to limit this increase as much as possible and prioritise sustainable urban transport solutions where these can be sustained by sufficient urban density and population. In addition, housing choices can be influenced by promoting compact cities. One option is to develop an integrated housing index taking both housing and transport costs into account, like the Housing and Transportation (H+T) Affordability Index in the United States. Such an index could be used by individuals to affect housing location choices and by planners to develop a plan to encourage the construction of affordable housing in neighbourhoods with higher land costs but lower transport costs, while focusing transit investments such that the amount that remote households spend on transport is reduced (Guerra and Kirschen, 2016[47]). Integrating housing and transport also contributes to avoiding segregation and facilitates access to public services and economic opportunities that could otherwise remain out of reach for these households due to a lack of suitable transport options. In both Olomouc and Pilsen, transport infrastructure is part of the land use plan elaborated at the municipal level. Better co-ordinating with surrounding municipalities or issuing guidelines for municipalities to follow when writing their land use plans could support these objectives.

Energy costs are also a very large factor when it comes to assessing housing affordability in cities in the Czech Republic. Low-income households that may already find it harder to find affordable housing are especially affected by what is known as energy poverty. Energy-poor households experience inadequate levels of essential energy services, including adequate warmth, cooling, lighting and the energy to power appliances, due to a combination of high energy expenditure, low household incomes, inefficient buildings and appliances, and specific household energy needs (EU Energy Poverty Observatory, n.d.[48]). High energy costs and energy poverty are a problem for housing affordability if households cannot afford to actually live in their home, as pointed out in Chapter 1. In the Czech Republic, lower-income households may be particularly affected because they cannot afford newer, more efficient appliances (Bouzarovski, 2014[49]). In addition, they often live in older, non-refurbished buildings (especially in urban areas) and pay significantly higher energy bills compared to people who live in energy-efficient buildings and who enjoy the same level of comfort. The poor energy efficiency of accommodation, low income and high energy bills can thus combine to make a vicious cycle in which energy poverty is aggravated (Ugarte et al., 2016[42]). As discussed in Chapter 1, urban residents in the Czech Republic are also more likely to face energy poverty, as households in cities, towns and suburbs are more likely to be unable to keep their house adequately warm than in rural areas. It is, therefore, necessary to focus on building refurbishment in cities, which helps increase the energy efficiency of buildings and can thus relieve part of the overburden currently put on energy-poor households.

The Czech Republic has established several subsidy schemes that reduce the energy consumption of buildings, partially in response to the EU Energy Efficiency Directive (Directive 2012/27/EU) that established a set of binding measures to help the EU reach its 20% energy efficiency target by 2020. In addition to SIPF-administered programmes to subsidise the installation of solar panels, the Czech Green Savings Programme focused primarily on supporting the insulation of buildings intended for permanent residence, as well as the use of renewable energy sources for space and water heating in households. The Ministry of the Environment's New Green Savings Programme is administered by the State Environmental Fund of the Czech Republic (n.d.[50]) and supports the following activities:

- Renovation of family houses and multi-unit buildings (thermal insulation of facade, roof and ceiling, replacement of windows and doors).
- Construction of family houses and multi-unit buildings in so-called passive housing standard (passive houses).
- Solar thermal and photovoltaic systems.
- Green roofs.
- Use of heat from wastewater.
- Controlled ventilation systems with heat recovery (recuperation).
- Replacement of heat sources for heat pumps, biomass boilers, etc.

While this programme aims to target the causes of energy poverty, it does not succeed in doing so as households affected by energy poverty do not have sufficient financial means to invest in them as subsidies are paid retroactively (Karásek and Pavlica, 2016[51]). Programmes to combat energy poverty must be affordable to households at risk of this type of poverty, for example by providing loans upfront. The programme must be incorporated into the national legislation and co-operate with existing support programmes for reducing energy consumption in buildings (Karásek and Pojar, 2018[52]).

The full impact of COVID-19 on energy-poor households will remain to be seen. However, preliminary findings have shown that energy consumption is expected to rise, both due to increased demand for conventional household tasks as more time is spent in the home (space heating, hot water, cooking and dishwashing) and new energy demands that come with teleworking (Mastropietro, Rodilla and Batlle, 2020[53]). Coupled with the contraction of the job market and increasing unemployment rates, many households have seen their income decline abruptly and may thus be at an increased risk of poverty. While energy poverty is only one dimension of poverty, providing more accessible programmes for households to lower their energy bills should be explored as a way to lower the financial burden of housing on households. Here, attention should be given to solutions that have been proven to be efficient both environmentally and financially, such as thermal insulation. One possible solution would be providing loans for thermal insulation to low-income households.

Cities have increasingly taken the issue of energy into their own hands. The city of Litoměřice, for example, introduced a local subsidy scheme for solar water heaters in 2000 as the first Czech city to do so and has recently even set up an Energy Efficiency Revolving Fund to trigger sustainable energy investments in public buildings (INNOVATE, n.d.[54]). The city was also one of the three founding members of a national association of municipalities concerned with energy efficiency. The Association of Energy Managers of Towns and Municipalities (SEMMO) now consists of 12 members (n.d.[55]). Although energy poverty is only one aspect of poverty, introducing schemes to lower the burden of energy costs should be encouraged, as long as they are accessible to all households.

Czech national and local governments could also tap into current and upcoming sources of financing in order to upgrade the existing housing stock in cities, such as those offered by the EU. In the context of the recovery package and the Renovation Wave,[6] the European Commission (EC) launched an Affordable Housing Initiative (AHI).[7] It will provide support, knowledge and expertise to local industrial partnerships with the ambition to pilot 100 lighthouse renovation districts in a smart neighbourhood approach embedded in locally-led development strategies, putting liveability, sustainability and socially responsible business models at the forefront. Liaising with other EU initiatives on urban development and regeneration such as the European Urban Initiative, the AHI will act as a co-ordination, networking and knowledge hub for industry, public authorities, financial institutions and key stakeholders in the social and affordable housing sector. It will share blueprints for the replication of successful lighthouse districts, as well as better and socially responsible regulation standards, governance and access to sustainable finance, skills and knowledge on complex financial combinations for local projects, deep renovation and neighbourhood approaches that could facilitate the renovation of social and affordable housing districts across the EU in the long run.

The AHI will launch in early 2022 and Czech authorities may benefit from entering an EU-level cross-sectoral partnership with representatives of the construction sector and (social) housing sector, including co-operatives and associations, social economy and civil society, and other public authorities. It will provide direct support to small- and medium-sized businesses, including social enterprises, to collaborate with local authorities and (social) housing providers, to integrate the latest digital, environmental and social innovative solutions targeting social and affordable housing and neighbourhood renovation, and to upskill and reskill. It will also help to mobilise funding opportunities for the renovation projects targeting social and affordable housing at the neighbourhood level to be implemented in the best conditions possible (the Recovery and Resilience Facility, cohesion funds, philanthropy, private capital, InvestEU, ELENA [European Local ENergy Assistance], etc.).

Joint planning of housing across municipal boundaries could be strengthened

Intermunicipal co-ordination on spatial planning and housing currently remains limited. This is for example the case in Pilsen, as surrounding municipalities are very small and compete to attract population. According to the OECD-MMR housing survey, only 30% of surveyed municipalities have a dedicated housing strategy and only 11% co-ordinate their housing policy with surrounding municipalities. While the responsibility for housing lies largely with Czech municipalities, these tend to be too small to provide cost-effective public services. Municipalities in the Czech Republic are extremely small and fragmented, both in terms of population (Figure 2.11) and in terms of surface. In particular, 89.2% of Czech municipalities have fewer than 2 000 inhabitants, which is a much higher share than the OECD average of 28.4%, with some municipalities having as little as tens of inhabitants.

Municipalities in the Czech Republic tend to compete for residents and therefore are reluctant to co-operate with neighbouring municipalities. Some of this can be traced back to the fiscal framework in place. Subnational governments in the Czech Republic are mostly financed through a mix of shared taxes (personal and corporate income tax and VAT) and grants and transfers from the central government. Although progressive decentralisation from 1989 onwards has given Czech municipalities more competencies, municipalities have little autonomy over their revenue as most taxes are shared. Municipalities in the Czech Republic therefore tend to compete with one another for the population in order to increase their revenue base and the size of government transfers, since population size is the main determinant of the revenues that municipalities receive from the national government through the tax-sharing formula. Such intermunicipal co-operation may lead to suboptimal land uses such as the promotion of sprawling housing developments for which it is costly to provide services and deliver and maintain infrastructure (OECD, 2017[35]).

Figure 2.11. Czech municipalities are the smallest in the OECD

Municipalities by population size class by country

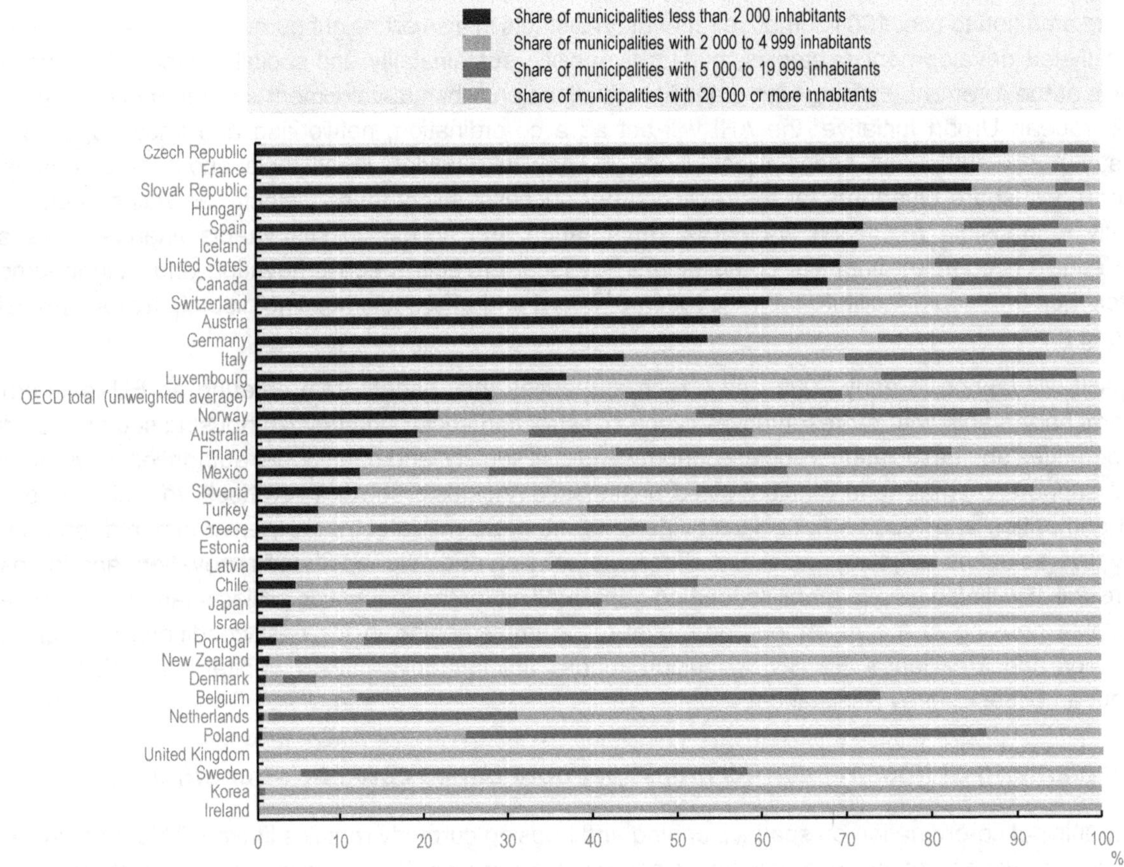

Source: OECD (2017[56]), OECD Regional Statistics Database: Subnational government structure and finance, OECD, Paris

The tax-sharing formula in the Czech Republic has been the subject of much debate. Each region's share of the overall allocation to regions is set in the legislation. For municipalities, revenues are strongly linked to the population size and only weakly linked to cost drivers and the local economy; there is therefore little reward for growing the tax base. The link in the tax-sharing formula to where revenue is raised could be strengthened further for regions and municipalities, accompanied by an explicit equalisation component to account for differences in a revenue-raising capacity (OECD, 2016[57]). Given the need for more intermunicipal co-operation, several OECD reports have noted that this formula could be better structured to acknowledge the differences in revenue-raising capacity among municipalities in order to enhance horizontal equity.

In addition to the issue of tax sharing, the OECD has long held the position that the Czech Republic is not using the property tax to its full advantage (2020[58]). At 0.6% of total government tax revenue in 2018, the recurrent tax on immovable property is very low compared to the OECD average of 3.1% (OECD, n.d.[59]). The same holds true for the subnational level: the property tax on land and buildings accounts for 4.3% of subnational government tax revenue, 2% of total consolidated subnational government revenue (Figure 2.12) and 0.2% of GDP, which is well below the OECD average of 1.1% of GDP (SNGWOFI, 2019[60]).

Figure 2.12. Subnational government revenue from the property tax is very low in the Czech Republic

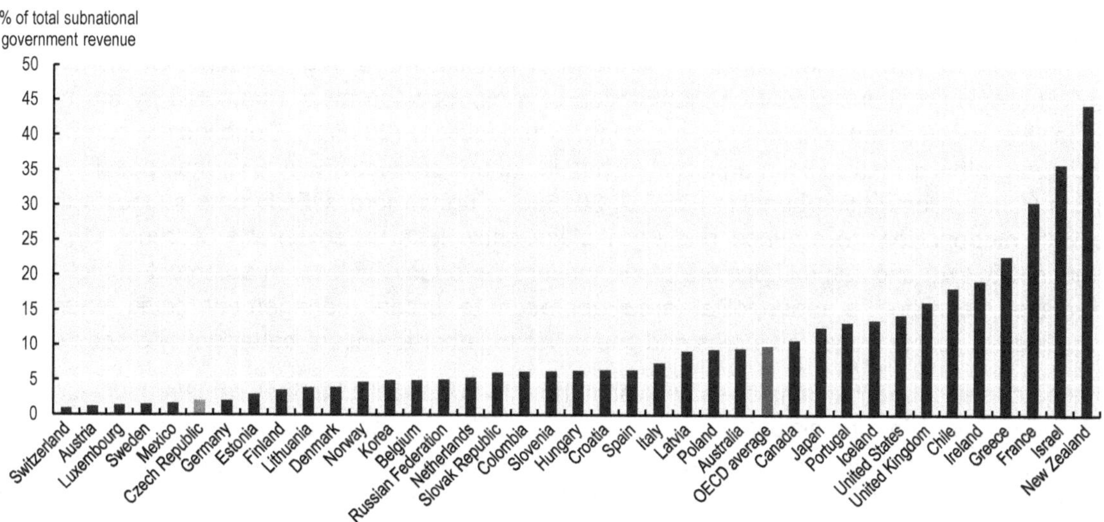

Source: OECD/UCLG (2020[61]), *OECD-UCLG World Observatory on Subnational Government Finance and Investment*, https://stats.oecd.org/viewhtml.aspx?datasetcode=SNGF_WO&vh=0000&vf=00&l&il=blank&lang=en&vcq=1111 (accessed on 10 April 2020).

Furthermore, differentiated property tax could be used to incentivise more efficient land use through higher-density housing development, discourage low-density housing and promote brownfield developments. Czech municipalities currently underuse these types of instruments and this is a missed opportunity. In particular, property tax does not capture changes in market value. Rather than allowing private individuals and businesses to retain the entire market value benefit from increased property values attributable to public spending and investment, municipalities in the Czech Republic could take steps to "capture" a portion of the increases in value. A shift to a value-based property tax and/or introducing various "value capture" mechanisms linked to specific public infrastructure projects would achieve such an objective.

Existing instruments such as the local coefficient for property tax could also be more effectively leveraged. In the wake of the financial crisis of 2007-08, municipalities gained some autonomy over their revenue by receiving the ability to introduce a "local coefficient" on real estate tax. While the base rate is set centrally, municipalities can raise the rate up to five times the minimum threshold amount. By adjusting the coefficient from 1 up to 5, municipalities are able to increase their revenues from taxes on immovable property up to five times the minimum threshold amount set by the national government. However, most municipalities tend to set their local property tax rate at the low level and only 8% of municipalities have made use of this possibility to increase tax rates (Janoušková and Sobotovičová, 2016[62]). However, in the municipalities that have taken advantage of setting their marginal rate higher than the threshold, higher revenues have been successfully used for service provision (Zdražil and Pernica, 2018[63]). Taking advantage of this local coefficient could help municipalities raise their tax revenues, thus enabling them to invest more money in housing and other public services, and should be strongly encouraged. Effective tax rates should be raised to increase the share of revenues that municipalities directly control. More importantly, the calculation should be based on property value rather than property size, with these values updated regularly, as in most OECD countries. However, care must be taken to avoid increasing the housing burden of low-income households. To avoid resistance from municipalities to increase the property tax rate and unintended consequences for vulnerable households, targeted means-tested exemptions, such as exemptions for low-income households, could be introduced.

Co-ordinating housing, land use and other sectors such as transport across municipal boundaries can increase efficiency and help avoid negative externalities such as urban sprawl. Because people cross administrative boundaries on a daily basis, often without realising it, policies of one municipality often spill over to affect those around them. For example, the effects of infrastructure projects are not limited to municipal boundaries and can generate externalities for neighbouring municipalities. The lack of co-ordination and co-operation may generate a cost for residents, businesses and subnational governments in the form of inefficiencies generated by administrative fragmentation. OECD data shows that a higher level of administrative fragmentation of a metropolitan area, measured by the number of municipalities, is correlated with lower levels of labour productivity (2015[64]). Doubling the number of local governments within a metropolitan area diminishes its labour productivity by 6%, thus possibly reducing the gains from agglomeration benefits (OECD, 2015[64]). Furthermore, OECD data suggests that urban areas with metropolitan governance bodies in place show less urban sprawl (Ahrend, Gamper and Schumann, 2014[65]) and can mitigate the aforementioned productivity loss. In a context of high territorial fragmentation, adopting a metropolitan-area approach to urban management could enable small municipalities to pool financial resources and capacities together to ensure better policy outcomes.

Various co-operation mechanisms already exist in the Czech Republic but they remain under-used in the domain of housing. Intermunicipal co-operation in the Czech Republic can take place through the 207 municipalities with extended power (*Obec s rozšířenou působností*) that were given the responsibilities of the former state districts when these were abolished in 2003. These municipalities with extended powers are larger municipalities that perform functions delegated by the central government for a particular catchment area. The central government finances these services through grants (Sedmihradská, 2018[66]). Smaller municipalities can also delegate additional functions to the municipalities with extended powers that they do not want to perform or are not able to perform because of their lack of capacities (OECD, 2019[67]). Other modes of co-operation among municipalities are promoted in the Czech Republic 2000 Act on Municipalities. Several different types of co-operation and co-ordination between municipalities exist, including "voluntary municipal associations", of which 731 were active in 2014 (Sedmihradská, 2018[66]). These can be founded by two or more neighbouring or non-neighbouring municipalities. The main areas of activity of voluntary municipal associations are water and sewage management, followed by waste management. The expenditure of voluntary municipal associations in the area of housing and communal services has increased in the past decade (Sedmihradská, 2018[66]) but there remains untapped potential for intermunicipal collaboration on housing within this framework. The lack of incentives for municipalities to pool resources could be overcome by implementing planning instruments at a larger scale that encompasses municipalities and their functional area (OECD, 2012[68]). The national government can continue providing incentives for intermunicipal co-operation and joint service provision, including contractual arrangements and financial transfers. One promising step towards a metropolitan strategy is that the 2015 Spatial Development Plan that tasks the MMR, the city of Prague and the Central Bohemia Region with conducting regional studies focused on regional infrastructure interaction, co-ordinating development and conducting territorial studies on suburbanisation and unsystematic development in the area (OECD, 2018[38]). More effective intermunicipal co-ordination on housing could help municipalities build economies of scale in the administration and maintenance of public housing.

Conclusion

As housing costs in cities in the Czech Republic continue to rise and the full extent of the social and economic fallout from the COVID-19 crisis remains uncertain, the Czech Republic must brace itself for an increased demand for affordable housing and act swiftly to keep housing affordable for its population, particularly in cities. The national government can do a lot to guide and harmonise social housing provision by municipalities, provide housing to the most vulnerable members of society and decrease the prevalence of dormitories in cities. However, housing affordability must also be addressed more broadly, by increasing access to the private rental market and encouraging construction in municipalities where housing prices are high. Joint planning across municipalities, aligning housing affordability objectives with other social and environmental objectives and deploying spatial and land use planning instruments strategically can also be powerful tools to tackle the affordability issue from different sides. Only through a concerted effort from all levels of government will the Czech Republic be able to improve housing affordability for all in cities.

References

Ahrend, R., C. Gamper and A. Schumann (2014), "The OECD Metropolitan Governance Survey: A Quantitative Description of Governance Structures in large Urban Agglomerations", *OECD Regional Development Working Papers*, No. 2014/4, OECD Publishing, Paris, https://dx.doi.org/10.1787/5jz43zldh08p-en. [65]

Boehm, T. and A. Schlottmann (1999), "Does home ownership by parents have an economic impact on their children?", *Journal of Housing Economics*, Vol. 8/3, pp. 217-232, https://ideas.repec.org/a/eee/jhouse/v8y1999i3p217-232.html (accessed on 26 February 2021). [13]

Bouzarovski, S. (2014), "Energy poverty in the European Union: Landscapes of vulnerability", *Wiley Interdisciplinary Reviews: Energy and Environment*, Vol. 3/3, pp. 276-289, http://dx.doi.org/10.1002/wene.89. [49]

Burchardt, T. and J. Hills (1998), "From public to private: The case of mortgage payment insurance in Great Britain", *Housing Studies*, Vol. 13/3, pp. 311-323, http://dx.doi.org/10.1080/02673039883308. [19]

Causa, O. and J. Pichelmann (2020), "Should I stay or should I go? Housing and residential mobility across OECD countries", *OECD Economics Department Working Papers*, No. 1626, OECD Publishing, Paris, https://doi.org/10.1787/d91329c2-en (accessed on 26 February 2021). [17]

Cournède, B., V. Ziemann and F. De Pace (2020), "The Future of Housing: Policy Scenarios", *OECD Economics Department Working Papers*, No. 1624, OECD Publishing, Paris, https://dx.doi.org/10.1787/0adf02cb-en. [31]

Czech Ministry of Transport (2013), *The Transport Policy of the Czech Republic for 2014-2020 with the Prospect of 2050*, https://www.dataplan.info/img_upload/7bdb1584e3b8a53d337518d988763f8d/b13-00298_ministerstvo_dopravy_2014_2020_eng-05_1.pdf (accessed on 3 June 2020). [44]

de Boer, R. and R. Bitetti (2014), "A Revival of the Private Rental Sector of the Housing Market?: Lessons from Germany, Finland, the Czech Republic and the Netherlands", *OECD Economics Department Working Papers*, No. 1170, OECD Publishing, Paris, https://dx.doi.org/10.1787/5jxv9f32j0zp-en. [6]

DiPasquale, D. and E. Glaeser (1999), "Incentives and social capital: Are homeowners better citizens?", *Journal of Urban Economics*, https://www.sciencedirect.com/science/article/pii/S0094119098920988 (accessed on 26 February 2021). [14]

EC (2020), *Country Report Czechia 2020: 2020 European Semester: Assessment of Progress on Structural Reforms, Prevention and Correction of Macroeconomic Imbalances, and Results of In-depth Reviews under Regulation (EU) No 1176/2011*, European Commission, https://eur-lex.europa.eu/legal-content/EN/TXT/PDF/?uri=CELEX:52020SC0502&from=EN. [26]

EC (2018), "Social housing pilot in Ostrava promotes inclusion in the Czech Republic", European Commission, https://ec.europa.eu/regional_policy/en/projects/czechia/social-housing-pilot-in-ostrava-promotes-inclusion-in-the-czech-republic. [27]

EC (n.d.), *Czech Republic - Employment, Social Affairs & Inclusion*, European Commission, https://ec.europa.eu/social/main.jsp?catId=1106&langId=en&intPageId=4470 (accessed on 30 April 2020). [8]

ECSR (2020), *European Federation of National Organisations Working with the Homeless (FEANTSA) v. Czech Republic Complaint No. 191/2020*, European Committee of Social Rights. [34]

EU Energy Poverty Observatory (n.d.), *What is Energy Poverty?*, https://www.energypoverty.eu/about/what-energy-poverty (accessed on 8 October 2020). [48]

EU Urban Agenda Housing Partnership (2017), *EU Urban Agenda-Housing Partnership Guidance Paper on EU Regulation & Public Support for Housing*, https://ec.europa.eu/futurium/sites/futurium/files/housing_partnership_-_guidance_paper_on_eu_regulation_and_public_support_for_housing_03-2017.pdf (accessed on 5 February 2021). [32]

European Commission (2020), *COMMUNICATION FROM THE COMMISSION TO THE EUROPEAN PARLIAMENT, THE COUNCIL, THE EUROPEAN ECONOMIC AND SOCIAL COMMITTEE AND THE COMMITTEE OF THE REGIONS: A Renovation Wave for Europe - greening our buildings, creating jobs, improving lives*, https://ec.europa.eu/energy/sites/ener/files/eu_renovation_wave_strategy.pdf. [70]

Fack, G. (2006), "Are housing benefit an effective way to redistribute income? Evidence from a natural experiment in France", *Labour Economics*, Vol. 13/6, pp. 747-771, http://dx.doi.org/10.1016/j.labeco.2006.01.001. [11]

Gibbons, S. and A. Manning (2006), "The incidence of UK housing benefit: Evidence from the 1990s reforms", *Journal of Public Economics*, Vol. 90/4-5, pp. 799-822, http://dx.doi.org/10.1016/j.jpubeco.2005.01.002. [10]

Guerra, E. and M. Kirschen (2016), "Housing Plus Transportation Affordability Indices: Uses, Opportunities, and Challenges", *International Transport Forum Discussion Papers*, No. 2016/14, OECD Publishing, Paris, https://dx.doi.org/10.1787/a1fc9b79-en. [47]

Heeckt, C. and O. Huerta (n.d.), "Building compact, connected and clean cities in Mexico: National housing and transport policy priorities", Coalition for Urban Transitions, London. [43]

INNOVATE (n.d.), *Litoměřice (Czech Republic) - Financing Building Renovation*, http://www.financingbuildingrenovation.eu/cases/litomerice-municipality-czech-republic/ (accessed on 11 June 2020). [54]

ITF (2019), *ITF Transport Outlook 2019*, OECD Publishing, Paris, https://dx.doi.org/10.1787/transp_outlook-en-2019-en. [45]

Janků, J. et al. (2016), "Estimation of land loss in the Czech Republic in the near future", *Soil and Water Research*, Vol. 11/3, pp. 155-162, http://dx.doi.org/10.17221/40/2016-SWR. [37]

Janoušková, J. and Š. Sobotovičová (2016), "Immovable property tax in the Czech Republic as an instrument of fiscal decentralization", *Technological And Economic Development Of Economy*, Vol. 22/6, pp. 767-782, http://dx.doi.org/10.3846/20294913.2016.1236355. [62]

Karásek, J. and J. Pavlica (2016), "Green investment scheme: Experience and results in the Czech Republic", *Energy Policy*, Vol. 90, pp. 121-130, http://dx.doi.org/10.1016/j.enpol.2015.12.020. [51]

Karásek, J. and J. Pojar (2018), "Programme to reduce energy poverty in the Czech Republic", *Energy Policy*, Vol. 115, pp. 131-137, http://dx.doi.org/10.1016/j.enpol.2017.12.045. [52]

Lam, J. (1985), "Type of structure, satisfaction and propensity to move", *Housing and Society*, Vol. 12/1, pp. 32-44, http://dx.doi.org/10.1080/08882746.1985.11429958. [16]

Lipej, B. and G. Turel (2018), "Housing cooperatives as an opportunity for solving the housing issue", *RELAND: International Journal of Real Estate & Land Planning*, Vol. 1/0, pp. 2623-4807, http://dx.doi.org/10.26262/RELAND.V1I0.6478. [33]

Lux, M. et al. (2017), "Reasoning behind choices: Rationality and social norms in the housing market behaviour of first-time buyers in the Czech Republic", *Housing Studies*, Vol. 32/4, pp. 517-539, http://dx.doi.org/10.1080/02673037.2016.1219331. [29]

Lux, M. and P. Sunega (2017), "Social housing in the Czech Republic: The change of a trend?", *Critical Housing Analysis*, Vol. 4/1, pp. 81-89, http://dx.doi.org/10.13060/23362839.2017.4.1.327. [25]

Lux, M. and P. Sunega (2012), "Labour mobility and housing", *Urban Studies*, Vol. 49/3, pp. 489-504, https://EconPapers.repec.org/RePEc:sae:urbstu:v:49:y:2012:i:3:p:489-504 (accessed on 26 February 2021). [20]

Lux, M. and P. Sunega (2010), "Private rental housing in the Czech Republic: Growth and...?", *Sociologický Časopis*, Vol. 46, pp. 349-373, http://dx.doi.org/10.2307/41132863. [30]

Macintyre, S. et al. (1998), "Do housing tenure and car access predict health because they are simply markers of income or self esteem? A Scottish study", *Journal of Epidemiology and Community Health*, Vol. 52/10, pp. 657-664, http://dx.doi.org/10.1136/jech.52.10.657. [15]

Mastropietro, P., P. Rodilla and C. Batlle (2020), "Measures to tackle the Covid-19 outbreak impact on energy poverty: Preliminary analysis based on the Italian and Spanish experiences", EU Energy Poverty Observatory, https://www.energypoverty.eu/publication/measures-tackle-covid-19-outbreak-impact-energy-poverty-preliminary-analysis-based (accessed on 4 June 2020). [53]

MMR (2018), *Housing in the Czech Republic in Figures*, Ministry of Regional Development of the Czech Republic, https://www.ohchr.org/Documents/Issues/Housing/Financialization/CzechRepublic2.pdf. [5]

MMR (2011), *Housing Policy Concept of the Czech Republic Till 2020*, State Housing Development Fund, Ministry of Regional Development of the Czech Republic, https://www.bmszki.hu/sites/default/files/fajlok/node-293/housing_policy_concept_till_2020.pdf (accessed on 30 March 2020). [3]

MMR (n.d.), "Main changes to the new law", Ministry of Regional Development of the Czech Republic, https://www.mmr.cz/cs/caste-dotazy/novy-stavebni-zakon/hlavni-zmeny-noveho-zakona (accessed on 30 April 2020). [40]

OECD (2021), "Building for a better tomorrow: Policies to make housing more affordable", *Employment, Labour and Social Affairs Policy Briefs*, OECD, Paris, http://oe.cd/affordable-housing-2021 (accessed on 26 February 2021). [1]

OECD (2021), *OECD Affordable Housing Database*, OECD, Paris, http://www.oecd.org/social/affordable-housing-database.htm. [7]

OECD (2020), "How's Life in the Czech Republic?", in *How's Life? 2020: Measuring Well-being*, OECD Publishing, Paris, https://dx.doi.org/10.1787/6b12022a-en. [24]

OECD (2020), *OECD Affordable Housing Database*, OECD, Paris. [22]

OECD (2020), *OECD Economic Surveys: Czech Republic 2020*, OECD Publishing, Paris, https://dx.doi.org/10.1787/1b180a5a-en. [58]

OECD (2019), *Making Decentralisation Work: A Handbook for Policy-Makers*, OECD Multi-level Governance Studies, OECD Publishing, Paris, https://dx.doi.org/10.1787/g2g9faa7-en. [67]

OECD (2019), "OECD Affordable Housing Database: Policy instruments and level of governance", OECD, Paris, https://www.oecd.org/els/family/PH1-1-Policy-instruments-levels-of-governance.pdf (accessed on 30 March 2020). [4]

OECD (2019), "OECD Affordable Housing Database: Recipients and payment rates of housing allowances", https://www.oecd.org/els/family/PH3-3-recipients-payment-rates-housing-allowances.pdf. [9]

OECD (2018), *OECD Environmental Performance Reviews: Czech Republic 2018*, OECD Environmental Performance Reviews, OECD Publishing, Paris, https://dx.doi.org/10.1787/9789264300958-en. [38]

OECD (2017), *OECD Regional Statistics Database: Subnational government structure and finance*, https://stats.oecd.org/Index.aspx?DataSetCode=SNGF (accessed on 1 June 2021). [56]

OECD (2017), *The Governance of Land Use in the Czech Republic: The Case of Prague*, OECD Publishing, Paris, https://dx.doi.org/10.1787/9789264281936-en. [35]

OECD (2016), *OECD Economic Surveys: Czech Republic 2016*, OECD Publishing, Paris, https://dx.doi.org/10.1787/eco_surveys-cze-2016-en. [57]

OECD (2015), *The Metropolitan Century: Understanding Urbanisation and its Consequences*, OECD Publishing, Paris, https://dx.doi.org/10.1787/9789264228733-en. [64]

OECD (2012), *Redefining "Urban": A New Way to Measure Metropolitan Areas*, OECD Publishing, Paris, https://dx.doi.org/10.1787/9789264174108-en. [68]

OECD (n.d.), *OECD Regional Statistics Database: Subnational government structure and finance*, https://stats.oecd.org/BrandedView.aspx?oecd_bv_id=region-data-en&doi=05fb4b56-en (accessed on 2 June 2020). [69]

OECD (n.d.), *OECD Stat: Greenhouse Gas Emissions*, OECD, Paris, https://stats.oecd.org/Index.aspx?DataSetCode=AIR_GHG (accessed on 4 June 2020). [46]

OECD (n.d.), *Revenue Statistics - OECD Countries: Comparative Tables*, OECD, Paris, https://stats.oecd.org/Index.aspx?DataSetCode=REV (accessed on 1 June 2020). [59]

OECD/MMR (2020), *OECD-MMR Housing Survey of Municipalities in the Czech Republic.* [23]

OECD/UCLG (2020), *OECD-UCLG World Observatory on Subnational Government Finance and Investment*, https://stats.oecd.org/viewhtml.aspx?datasetcode=SNGF_WO&vh=0000&vf=00&l&il=blank&lang=en&vcq=1111 (accessed on 10 April 2020). [61]

OECD/UN-Habitat (2018), *Global State of National Urban Policy*, OECD Publishing, Paris/United Nations Human Settlements Programme, Nairobi, https://dx.doi.org/10.1787/9789264290747-en. [2]

Office of the Government (2019), *2019 European Semester: National Reform Programme of the Czech Republic 2019*, https://ec.europa.eu/info/sites/info/files/2019-european-semester-national-reform-programme-czech-republic_en.pdf. [28]

Oswald, A. (1996), *A Conjecture on the Explanation for High Unemployment in the Industrialized Nations: Part I*, https://ageconsearch.umn.edu/record/268744/ (accessed on 26 February 2021). [18]

Petřík, P., J. Fanta and M. Petrtýl (2015), "It is time to change land use and landscape management in the czech republic", *Ecosystem Health and Sustainability*, Vol. 1/9, pp. 1-6, http://dx.doi.org/10.1890/15-0016.1. [36]

Rohe, W. and M. Stegman (1994), "The effects of homeownership: On the self-esteem, perceived control and life satisfaction of low-income people", *Journal of the American Planning Association*, Vol. 60/2, pp. 173-184, http://dx.doi.org/10.1080/01944369408975571. [21]

Sedmihradská, L. (2018), "Inter-municipal cooperation in the Czech Republic: A public finance perspective", *NISPAcee Journal of Public Administration and Policy*, Vol. 11/2, pp. 153-170, http://dx.doi.org/10.2478/nispa-2018-0017. [66]

SEMMO (n.d.), *About Us*, Association of Energy Managers of Cities and Municipalities, https://semmo.cz/o-nas/ (accessed on 11 June 2020). [55]

Shoup, D. (2017), *The High Cost of Free Parking*, Routledge, http://dx.doi.org/10.4324/9781351179782. [41]

Sirovátka, T., R. Jahoda and I. Malý (2019), *ESPN Thematic Report on National Strategies to Fight Homelessness and Housing Exclusion – Czech Republic*, European Social Policy Network (ESPN), European Commission, Brussels. [12]

SNGWOFI (2019), *Country Profile: Czech Republic*, World Observatory on Subnational Government Finance and Investment, http://www.sng-wofi.org/country-profiles/ (accessed on 10 April 2020). [60]

State Environmental Fund ČR (n.d.), *New Green Savings Programme – SFŽP ČR*, State Environmental Fund of the Czech Republic, https://www.sfzp.cz/en/administered-programmes/new-green-savings-programme/ (accessed on 4 June 2020). [50]

Ugarte, S. et al. (2016), *Energy Efficiency for Low-Income Households: Study for the ITRE Committee*, European Parliament Directorate General for Internal Policies, https://www.europarl.europa.eu/RegData/etudes/STUD/2016/595339/IPOL_STU(2016)595339_EN.pdf (accessed on 4 June 2020). [42]

World Bank Group (2020), *Doing Business 2020: Economy Profile Czech Republic*, https://www.doingbusiness.org/content/dam/doingBusiness/country/c/czech-republic/CZE.pdf (accessed on 30 April 2020). [39]

Zdražil, P. and B. Pernica (2018), "Property tax and quality of life in the Czech municipalities: Does the policy of raising local coefficient imply potential or risk for development?", *Review Of Economic Perspectives – Národohospodářský Obzor*, Vol. 18/2, pp. 123–136, http://dx.doi.org/10.2478/revecp-2018-0007. [63]

Notes

[1] While interest rates and macroprudential regulations are beyond the scope of this report, they constitute important factors in determining housing demand and housing prices (OECD, 2020[58]).

[2] A family's decisive income is the sum of incomes of all of its members after deduction of contributions to health and social insurance and income tax. Decisive income therefore includes all earnings (employment, self-employment, loans, etc.), as well as some social benefits, such as child allowance and parental allowance.

[3] Based on responses from 219 municipalities (excluding municipalities that indicate that more than 30% of the total housing stock is municipally owned and provided at below market rates to remove outliers).

[4] Excluding municipalities that indicate that more than 30% of the total housing stock is social housing.

[5] Based on a sample of 59 municipalities that provided information on the number of housing units built.

[6] COM (2020)662 final of 14 October 2020 (European Commission, 2020[70]).

[7] See page 22 of COM (2020)662 final of 14 October 2020 (European Commission, 2020[70]).

Annex A. The OECD-MMR housing survey of municipalities in the Czech Republic

Overview

In co-operation with the Ministry of Regional Development of the Czech Republic (MMR), the OECD carried out a survey of 1 877 Czech municipalities in August/September 2020 to collect data on the housing market and housing policies at the municipal level. The survey covered all municipalities within functional urban areas (FUAs) of more than 50 000 inhabitants as defined by the OECD,[1] as well as the municipalities within the FUAs of Jablonec and Mladá Boleslav. A total of 871 municipalities (corresponding to 46.5% of all surveyed municipalities) responded to the survey as of 15 October 2020. Figure A A.1 shows the municipalities covered by the survey and their response status.

Figure A A.1. 2020 OECD-MMR housing survey on municipalities in the Czech Republic: geographical coverage and response status

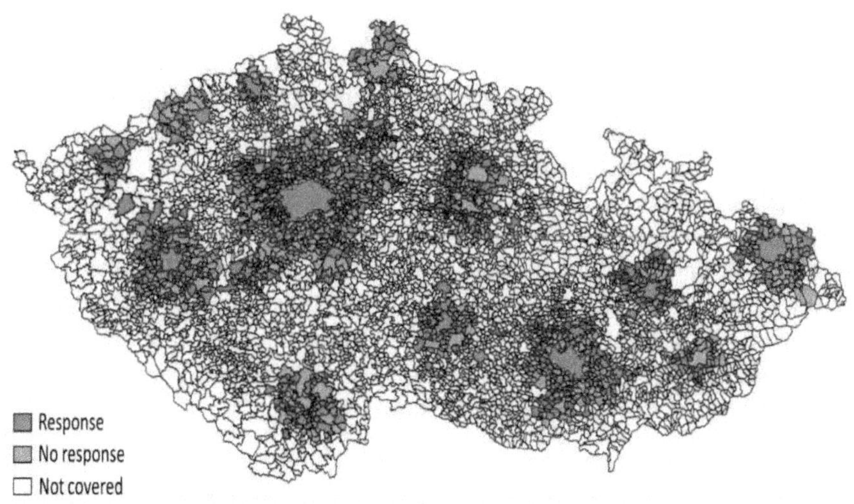

Source: OECD/MMR (2020[1]), *OECD-MMR Housing Survey of Municipalities in the Czech Republic.*

The survey collected detailed data on local housing markets, local housing policies and local land use regulations. It focused primarily on the following aspects:

- Housing stock, housing prices and land prices.
- Municipal and social housing.
- Housing policy framework.
- Land use regulations and planning policies (zoning by land use, density regulations, regulatory plans and the permitting process).
- Housing construction and constraints for residential development.

The survey aimed to collect data that is internationally comparable, while still capturing all important aspects of local housing and land use policies. Therefore, it contained sections that were designed to be applicable across countries, as well as sections that were targeted specifically at the Czech context. The survey instrument consisted of approximately 100 closed-ended questions.

Administration of the survey

The OECD-MMR housing survey was administered to local government officials on an online platform, by an external Czech survey provider. The objective was to receive one set of answers per surveyed municipality. If available, the survey provider contacted a specific official within a municipality and, otherwise, the municipality through generic contact details. Local officials and municipalities were contacted by postal mail, email and phone on behalf of the OECD and the Czech national government. When no response was received from municipalities, the survey provider sent up to four reminders to increase the response rate. Respondents were given one month in total to fill in their answers independently on the online platform.

Two different versions of the survey instrument were administered depending on the type of municipalities. Municipalities with extended powers – which fulfil administrative functions for assigned municipalities without extended powers – had to complete the full survey, including specific questions on their extended competencies, while municipalities without extended powers answered a reduced set of questions. The survey, moreover, instructed to provide the latest available information, up to March 2020. The survey was administered in Czech.

Survey data

The 871 municipalities that responded to the survey are home to 2.8 out of 6 million inhabitants in the Czech Republic. Overall, responding municipalities were representative of the surveyed municipalities in the sense that there was no difference in population and age structure among responding and non-responding municipalities. Thus, no correction was done to account for potential biases when calculating municipality level statistics. However, within FUAs, there were instances where there existed bias when comparing the responding and non-responding groups. As FUA level statistics are an aggregation of municipal-level data, information for municipalities that did not respond to the survey was partially extrapolated from the answers that other municipalities that did respond provided, together with external data observable for all municipalities. Thus, the data presented in the following may differ somewhat from data that is obtained from other data sources. In addition, the survey data was cleaned through statistical means to account for erroneous answers and implausible values.

The survey aimed to collect information that is not available in the Czech statistical system with a view to supporting the formulation of housing policy recommendations. It does not claim to replace official statistics but to complement them. In the case where no official statistics were available to support the answers to this survey, respondent municipalities were invited to provide approximate answers to the best of their knowledge.

Note

[1] The European Commission and the OECD have jointly developed a methodology to define FUAs in a consistent way across countries. Using population density and travel-to-work flows as key information, an FUA consists of a densely inhabited city and of a surrounding area (commuting zone) whose labour market is highly integrated with the city (Dijkstra, Poelman and Veneri, 2019[2]). The ultimate aim of the EC-OECD approach to FUAs is to create a harmonised definition of cities and their areas of influence for international comparison as well as for policy analysis on topics related to urban development.

www.ingramcontent.com/pod-product-compliance
Lightning Source LLC
LaVergne TN
LVHW081410110826
845149LV00010B/1696

* 9 7 8 9 2 6 4 4 2 9 7 0 3 *